THE COURSE CREATOR'S PLAYBOOK

RAY BREHM

and 18 successful course creators

THE COURSE CREATOR'S PLAYBOOK

THE SUCCESS PLAYBOOK SERIES

RAY BREHM

CONTRIBUTORS

Ray Brehm, Ryan Sullivan, Stella Marie Egbuji, Paula Judith Johnson, Carol L. Monson DO. MS, Barb Grant, J.K. Winn, Michele L. Whetzel, Sally Saxon JD, Bert A. Amsing, Sue Humphrey, Linda Berry, Ram Sharma, Ted Demopoulos, Robert Wood Anderson, Paul T Neustrom, Araba Afenyi-Annan, Shihan Sheriff and Erneste Carla Zimmermann.

CONTENTS

DONE IS BETTER THAN PERFECT

BY RAY BREHM

When it comes to creating a course, or anything else for that matter, there is always one roadblock.

If you are like me, you worry about releasing a less-than-perfect product. That can mean endless loops of tweaking, procrastination, and worry. And that is definitely a valid concern.

There is something worse though. Not sharing your knowledge with the world. The people who could use your help are not getting it while you are nitpicking yourself.

This applies whether you are writing a book, creating a course, or planning a coaching program. Or any of the other ways you may plan to deliver your knowledge.

It all comes down to one prevailing truth.

Those who would learn from you are not judging you based on your method of delivery. The vast majority don't care how much of an expert you are on that delivery. They care only if you know the subject you are teaching.

If you write a book on yoga, you don't have to be an expert writer. You only need to be an expert on yoga. If you want to create a digital course on yoga, you don't have to be a master course creator. Focus only on the yoga.

Which brings us to our theme. Done is better than perfect.

My personal mantra for following this guideline is this.

I strive to get to "version two" of everything I do as quickly as possible.

Nothing will ever be perfect, and I will make it better with each iteration. But I cannot even start that process until I get the first version done.

If you are writing a book, the most critical milestone is getting the rough draft done. From there, it is releasing the first version of your book.

When it comes to course creation, the same rules apply. Perhaps even more so.

You must release the beta version, or version one, or whatever you want to call it, as soon as possible.

Fortunately, for course creators, there is an incredible way to do that.

Create a pilot program.

My definition of a pilot course is one that you co-create with your students in real time. That means you sell the course but teach the first one live. That is your version one.

There are some incredible benefits to this.

- You skip past the procrastination stage and map out your course.
- Your students co-create the course with you. So, you will learn what is easy to learn and what takes more time. There will always be blind spots because you are so familiar with the material.
- When you teach live, you build relationships with your students. Some may need more help from you later.
- You get paid to create your course.

Let's review these with an example.

When I first launched my flagship course, Summit Lab, I used the pilot method. I had been running a Done-For-You Virtual Summit program for almost two years. I was confident in my expertise, but I was not 100% sure how to teach what I knew in a digital course format.

I also didn't want to spend months building it if I was only going to sell a few copies. So I sold it first.

How did I do that?

I mapped out the benefits of hosting a virtual summit (which are pretty incredible). They include building an audience to launch things like...

surprise, surprise... digital courses.

I also listed the topics and modules, and the order in which I would teach them, including the live dates.

And here is one of the keys to pilot programs. I told them it was a pilot, that there would be mistakes and live pivots in the material. But I stressed that it was a good thing; in fact, the benefits of participating in the pilot were substantial.

- There was more personal access to me via the live training and via email. That meant brainstorming ideas for summit themes. Also, it meant sharing how I run my summits.
- The price would be less than in the future, but they would have more of my time than future course releases.
- Live versions allow for questions and extra explanations.

The only thing I asked in return was that they tolerate any errors, typos, and the nature of the live training. They could even skip the live part. They would have lifetime access to the recordings and future updates to them.

The results for my situation were outstanding. I priced the pilot course at $497. I let them know it would rise to $997 or $1,497 in the future. That added some urgency.

I sold seven.

By announcing my pilot, I was paid nearly $3,500 to create my flagship program. Better yet, the students guided me on what topics they needed the most help with. This was better than my guessing while creating the course in advance.

Many of those pilot students went on to launch new businesses after hosting summits. Some of them became trusted partners of mine. That would not have occurred had I let procrastination rule the day.

But something else happened. Some students needed more help than others. The course helped others realize that their time might be better spent hiring me. So they inquired.

It was not my intent at the start. But, within 90 days after the pilot, I made an extra $28,000 in done-for-you and done-with-you summit services.

As a disclaimer, you should not expect the same kind of numbers. But *how much would you be willing to accept as payment for creating your course? Is that number possible?*

Before you start, list it for sale and see how much you can earn. If you sell too few copies, you can always cancel and return the money. But I bet you won't.

When I launched my version two of Summit Lab, I decided to teach that live as well.

Why?

The live teaching relationships were priceless for their connection, feedback, and lasting bonds.

Whenever I plan to create a new product or service instead of procrastinating, I sell a pilot. It is the best way to launch programs quickly. It ensures that the course has everything the students need.

And all you need to understand is that done is better than perfect.

Ray Brehm is USA Today and Wall Street Journal Bestselling Author, and the founder of Pubfunnels™, the #1 Business Hub For Authors. You can connect with Ray at <u>raybrehm.com</u> *or* learn about Pubfunnels at <u>pubfunnels.com</u>.

2

LESS X'S, MORE O'S

BY RYAN SULLIVAN

"You don't get paid for the hour; you get paid for the value you bring to the hour."

— JIM ROHN

Courses are like any other online product; people buy them based on perceived value. As an expert in your niche, creating that value seems simple enough: write content you would want to read, make videos you would want to watch, and create a product you would want to buy. Add tons of high-quality content, and the value will go up.

The reality is this couldn't be farther from the truth. Piling up the depth and breadth of content often leads to less value, not more. Understanding the true principles of course value creation can help you sell more courses, for higher prices than would otherwise be possible. To do so, you must realize that people will pay money for courses that provide them with one of three things:

- Efficiency (Speed to Goal).
- Expertise (Certainty of Success).
- Experience (Exclusivity of Participation).

Your course must provide one or all of these things to be successful. Providing efficiency or speed will help students to obtain their goal faster. Expertise provides credibility and authority to your offerings, instilling confidence and certainty of the outcome they seek. Finally, experiences add a layer of engagement for those seeking interactivity that they may not get through other similar courses.

Provide a course with efficiency, expertise, and experience, and you will unlock the secrets to crafting courses that sell with ease. The following will describe how to feature those qualities in your courses.

Efficiency (Speed to Goal)

"The only thing that beats 'free' is 'fast.' People will pay for speed."

— ALEX HORMOZI

The goal of your course design should not only be to make your lessons effective for your students but also efficient.

Your students purchase courses because they do not have the time to do the research themselves and find the best method on their own. Provide them with speed to action and problem resolution, and you will have a lifelong client coming back for more courses. Here is how to achieve that:

Make it Simpler

"If you can't explain it simply, you don't know it well enough!"

— ALBERT EINSTEIN

The biggest mistake that course creators often make is believing that adding more content means more value. It often doesn't solve problems; it creates them. Sometimes more information simply means more confusion. The chaos of ideas this information overload brings can lead to overwhelm, ultimately slowing down the students' understanding and speed to execution. As a result, they often don't know which of the possible steps to take next—or even worse, they take no action at all.

Your job as a course creator is to make sense of the chaos in the minds of your students and bring clarity and purpose to their actions. Simplify your content by distilling complex concepts into clear, concise language and operational steps. In other words, make it simple. Focus on delivering key insights and actionable takeaways that align with the goal of the course. By prioritizing simplicity, you make it easier for your audience to understand, retain, and execute the information you provide.

Make it Smaller

"The key to mastering any skill is to break it down into manageable parts and practice consistently."

— JIM KWIK

Large chunks of content can be daunting and overwhelming for learners. You have probably bought a course before that had an amazing sales page listing thirty items you were going to learn in the course, only to get inside and realize that those needles of wisdom were strewn throughout a three-hour webinar presentation haystack. The teaching points may be simple, but if your students can't easily get to them, now or in the future, they are worthless.

Instead, organize content into bite-sized modules or lessons, each focusing on a specific topic or learning objective for easier navigation and consumption. Breaking down complex concepts into digestible chunks empowers the learner to achieve their goals with minimal effort and maximum impact. Making specific content also allows for flexible editing or updating and helps niche down your target market to a specific client avatar to aid in course marketing.

Make it Diverse

"You don't understand anything until you learn it more than one way."

— MARVIN MINSKY

While it may seem obvious, everyone does not learn the same way. Some like reading text, others prefer watching videos, and others simply want condensed takeaways. To accommodate these various learning styles, incorporate different content formats such as videos, interactive quizzes, and downloadable resources in addition to the normal written content. Alternating methods of instruction also ensures that the material is presented in an engaging manner rather than repeating the same content methods.

Bonus materials, such as ebooks, checklists, or exclusive access to other content, not only serve as alternate learning options but also add extra value to your course. This multifaceted approach can ultimately lead to more robust comprehension and retention of knowledge.

Expertise (Certainty of Success)

"Excellence always sells."

— EARL NIGHTINGALE

Speed to execution may be enough to get some to buy, but others are willing to take any necessary time to invest in a product as long as they know it will work. This certainty, based on your expertise, past success, or guarantee, can be the ticket to consistent sales. But how do you establish your brand authority and differentiate yourself from all the other similar courses in your niche?

Make it Your Story

"An expert is a person who has made all the mistakes that can be made in a very narrow field."

— NIELS BOHR

Your story is your greatest asset, so be sure to include your individual experiences. Your story adds authenticity to your teachings, making them more relatable and engaging. Knowing you experienced the same problem, and have a unique solution that works, can motivate your students to see that they can achieve the same success.

Infusing your course with your personal narrative and life experiences provides your unique perspective that differentiates it from any other course. It is your anecdotes, insights, and lessons learned along your journey that provide the connection with your audience. Some will buy additional courses just to learn more through you. By leveraging your unique strengths, you establish yourself as a trusted guide that understands their problems and can help bring them to the other side with success.

Make it Applicable

"The past is where you learned the lesson. The future is where you apply the lesson. Don't give up in the middle."

— TRACY MALONE

Relevance is the currency of education. To be of value, it needs to be applicable. In other words, the opposite of that inverse tangent formula that you learned in high school math. While some topics can be timeless, the more specific your niche or training, the more likely it is that the content can become irrelevant or out of date if it is not maintained or updated. So, whenever you can, incorporate current examples, various case studies, and relevant lessons to demonstrate the real-world applicability of your teachings. If they can see themselves in your solution, it will ensure a higher rate of success.

Make it Actionable

"The value of an idea is in the use of it."

— THOMAS EDISON

Knowledge without action is like a seed without soil, never growing to its true potential. Actionable content equips your students with practical skills and knowledge they can immediately apply in their lives, driving instant results. Too often, courses describe the what but not the how, leaving the client inspired but unable to obtain any meaningful traction. Make your course content actionable by providing practical strategies, tools, and exercises that students can immediately implement. Empower your students to apply what they've learned to see tangible results, reinforcing their confidence and motivation to continue their learning journey with you.

Experience (Exclusivity of Participation)

"People don't buy for logical reasons. They buy for emotional reasons."

— ZIG ZIGLAR

Your course can have the most relevant expertise-driven solution for execution in the shortest time frame, but even then, some will not be able to execute on their own. Whether it is a live experience, a more intimate interactive group session, or the emotional high of a live event or gamified online community, these upgrades will ensure that your course not only educates your audience but also leads them to take inspired action.

Make it Interactive

"Tell me and I forget. Teach me and I remember. Involve me and I learn."

— BENJAMIN FRANKLIN

Providing options for self-paced learning works great for those who prefer to work on their own, but consider adding live sessions as well for those who thrive in interactive environments. Offering flexibility in content delivery allows your students to engage with the material in a way that best suits their individual preferences. Providing various course opportunities is essential for engaging students and ensuring they have a positive learning experience. Live sessions also allow for timely feedback on assignments, provide an avenue for students to seek clarification when they need it most, and help hold learners accountable and motivate them to stay on track with their studies.

Make it a Community

"I love being around people who are filled with exciting ideas, naive about what they don't know, and are willing to work."

— NOAH KAGAN

Allowance for continual interaction among a group of students in the same space and place in their journey provides a sense of community by encouraging interaction and collaboration. This is achieved through a variety of means like discussion forums, group projects, or coworking sessions. Emphasis on engagement and joint effort fosters a sense of belonging and can often mean the difference between simply reading text and actually executing your plan. By creating an interactive learning environment, you not only educate but also inspire your audience to become active participants in their own learning journey.

Make it Inspirational

"People will forget what you said, people will forget what you did, but people will never forget how you made them feel."

— MAYA ANGELOU

Sometimes it is not enough to simply give actionable steps, solutions, and advice. People want motivation and inspiration to execute their goals. Inspirational content can be recorded as examples of transformation based on your course or live motivational events built into your execution plan. It can also simply be an offer of ongoing support or resources to provide timely inspiration in those moments of struggle. You could also acknowledge and celebrate student progress and achievements at various points throughout the course, recognize milestones such as completing modules, mastering difficult concepts, or reaching personal goals, or you could celebrate these accomplishments with the group to inspire continued engagement and motivation.

With these principles in mind, you can design a course that not only meets the needs of your audience by consistently delivering value but also leaves a lasting impact on their lives.

So, demonstrate your value by using this method:

Provide **EFFICIENCY** and speed through clarity and purpose by **Making it Simpler**, breaking down content into manageable parts for easier navigation and comprehension by **Making it Smaller,** and catering to different learning styles with various content formats by **Making it Diverse.**

Demonstrate your **EXPERTISE** and provide certainty of success as you **Make it Your Story** by incorporating personal experiences to add authenticity and engagement, **Make it Applicable** by ensuring it remains relevant and valuable to your client base, and **Make it Actionable** by providing practical strategies and exercises for immediate application.

Finally, give them the **EXPERIENCE** and exclusivity of participation by **Making it Interactive** through live sessions and interactive features for engagement, **Making it a Community** by fostering collaboration and interaction among learners, and **Making it Inspirational** by providing ongoing motivation and support for transformative experiences.

Ryan is a veteran entrepreneur, business strategist, and marketing mentor who works with online directory and membership site owners looking for training, advice, and tools needed to succeed at their stage of growth. If you are looking to convert your marketplace potential, you can reach Ryan at DirectoryCourses.com

3

EMBRACING THE FEAR IN FAILURE: AN AUTHOR'S JOURNEY TO CREATING AN ONLINE COURSE

BY STELLA MARIE EGBUJI

The creation of an online course is a journey filled with excitement, innovation, and, inevitably, fear. As an author currently navigating the intricate process of developing a course called Embracing the Fear in Failure, I've come to understand the profound impact that addressing failure openly can have on learners.

Online education has seen explosive growth in recent years, with the global e-learning market projected to reach $336.98 billion by 2026, according to Research and Markets. This statistic reflects a growing recognition of the value and convenience of online learning platforms. However, the success of an online course hinges not only on market trends but also on the depth and authenticity of its content.

From the outset, my objective was to create a course that goes beyond traditional learning paradigms. I wanted to address the often-taboo subject of failure and its accompanying fear—a topic that resonates deeply with many but is seldom tackled head-on. In the words of Winston Churchill, "Success is not final; failure is not fatal. It is the courage to continue that counts." This quote became a guiding principle in my course design, as it emphasizes resilience and growth over perfection.

Understanding my target audience was crucial in shaping the course content. Who are these individuals? What fears do they harbor? How can they transform their apprehension of failure into a driving force for success? These questions formed the foundation of my research. According to a study by the Online Learning Consortium, 85 percent of students who have taken online courses feel that they are as good as, or better than, traditional classroom courses. This insight bolstered my confidence about the potential reach and impact of my course.

Creating an online course also demands a robust technological framework. High-quality video content, interactive exercises, and real-life case studies were integral components of my curriculum. This multimedia approach aimed to create an immersive learning experience. Additionally, research by Brandon Hall Group found that e-learning typically requires 40 to 60 percent less employee time than traditional learning, showcasing the efficiency and appeal of online education.

One of the primary challenges I faced was keeping the content engaging and relatable. In an online setting, where distractions are numerous, maintaining student engagement is paramount. To counteract this, I incorporated personal anecdotes and stories of renowned individuals who have turned their failures into successes. J.K. Rowling once said, "It is impossible to live without failing at something, unless you live so cautiously that you might as well not have lived at all—in which case, you fail by default." Such quotes and stories served as powerful reminders of the value of embracing failure.

Interactive elements like quizzes, reflection prompts, and peer discussion forums were included to foster active participation and a sense of community among learners. This approach aligns with Benjamin Franklin's wisdom: "Tell me and I forget. Teach me and I remember. Involve me and I will learn." By involving learners in the process, I aimed to facilitate deeper understanding and personal growth.

Continuous feedback and course improvement were vital components of my development process. The digital nature of online courses allows for real-time feedback through surveys and discussion forums. This iterative process enabled me to refine the content based on learner input, ensuring that the course remained relevant and impactful. According to a report by Docebo, companies that implement e-learning tools and strategies can boost productivity by up to 50 percent. This statistic highlights the importance of adaptability and responsiveness in online education.

One of the biggest obstacles to embracing failure is overcoming the stigma associated with it. In many cultures and industries, failure is often seen as a negative mark on one's record. However, research shows that this perspective is slowly shifting. According to a study by the Harvard Business Review, 84 percent of executives believe that failure is essential to innovation. This shift is crucial for fostering an environment where learning from mistakes is encouraged and valued.

To tackle this stigma head-on in my course, I incorporated examples from various industries. For instance, in the tech industry, failure is often celebrated as a stepping stone to success. Thomas Edison, one of the greatest inventors in history, is famously quoted as saying, "I have not failed. I've just found 10,000 ways that won't work." This mindset is a cornerstone of innovation and is something I strive to instill in my students.

Furthermore, I included insights from research on the benefits of failure. A study by Northwestern University found that early-career failures can lead to greater long-term success. The study revealed that scientists who experienced early-career rejections were more likely to publish high-impact papers later in their careers compared to those who did not face similar rejections. This statistic underscores the importance of perseverance and resilience in the face of failure.

To provide practical value, my course includes a range of strategies to help learners embrace failure. One effective approach is the concept of "fail fast, fail forward." This strategy encourages individuals to quickly identify and learn from their mistakes, using each failure as a stepping stone toward eventual success.

I also emphasize the importance of reflection and self-assessment. Encouraging learners to regularly reflect on their experiences and identify lessons learned from their failures can lead to significant personal and professional growth. Journaling, peer discussions, and mentorship are some of the tools I suggest for this reflective process.

Creating a supportive community is crucial for helping learners embrace failure. In my course, I focus on building a safe space where students can share their experiences, discuss their fears, and support each other. According to a report by the International Review of Research in Open and Distributed Learning, online learning communities can significantly enhance student engagement and satisfaction.

I incorporated discussion forums, live Q&A sessions, and peer-review activities to foster a sense of community. These interactive elements allow learners to connect with each other, share their failures, and celebrate their successes. As Aristotle once said, "The whole is greater than the sum of its parts." By building a supportive community, we can create an environment where learners feel empowered to take risks and learn from their failures.

In a recent survey by LinkedIn Learning, 61 percent of professionals stated that learning from their failures was the most valuable aspect of their career development. This aligns with my course's core message: Failure is not an end, but a critical component of growth and success. By embracing and learning from failure, we can foster resilience and innovation.

Psychologist Carol Dweck, known for her work on the "growth mindset," emphasizes that seeing failure as a learning opportunity rather than a setback can significantly enhance one's ability to succeed. Her research indicates that individuals who adopt a growth mindset are more likely to embrace challenges, persist in the face of setbacks, and achieve higher levels of success. This perspective is integral to the framework of my course, encouraging learners to reframe their understanding of failure.

As an author and educator, my goal is to demystify failure and help learners harness its potential. By providing practical strategies, inspirational stories, and a supportive learning environment, I aim to transform fear into a catalyst for personal and professional growth. The journey of creating this online course has been as much about my own learning and growth as it has been about preparing to teach others. Through this process, I have come to truly appreciate the wisdom in Samuel Beckett's words: "Ever tried. Ever failed. No matter. Try again. Fail again. Fail better."

One last piece of advice: You don't need to commission someone to create an online course. I realized this fact while creating Embracing the Fear in Failure. It was birthed from my personal and professional experience. While statistics on the percentage of online courses created from personal experience are not available, surveys suggest that a significant portion of creators leverage their own expertise and experiences. For example, a Teachable survey found that 83 percent of course creators design content based on personal skills and knowledge. Additionally, a LinkedIn Learning report noted that professionals increasingly seek to share their unique insights through online courses, contributing to the diverse range of topics available.

In conclusion, creating my online course, Embracing the Fear in Failure, has been a transformative experience. The ability to reach a global audience, coupled with the opportunity to address a universally relevant topic, makes this endeavor deeply rewarding. As I continue to refine and expand the course, I am reminded of Nelson Mandela's words: "Education is the most powerful weapon which you can use to change the world." Through this online course, I hope to equip learners with the tools to face their fears, embrace failure, and ultimately, achieve their fullest potential.

Stella Marie Egbuji is a Prayer Intercessor and an AWAI verified copywriter in Editorial/Content marketing copywriter, Lead Generation and Online Ad copywriter.

4

OUTCOME-FOCUSED COURSES
BY PAULA JUDITH JOHNSON

In today's competitive online course world, creating information products is not enough to entice adult learners to part with their hard-earned money.

According to Google, various research indicates that adult students complete only 5 to 15 percent of online courses. In fact, ResearchGate puts the completion rate for massive open online courses at only 3 to 6 percent.

As an online course creator, how do you craft a course that engages students so they are 1) disinclined to request a refund, and 2) inspired to complete the course?

Most adults today lack either the time or the curiosity to learn just for the sake of learning. Instead, they have a goal in mind when taking online courses. They want the time and money investment to pay off with a lasting impact related to the subject matter.

For instance, a novice or newer fiction author may have

the goal of writing an award-winning novel. They probably know a few basics about writing fiction and may even have a completed manuscript. There are a number of writing techniques that can be taught to assist this fledgling author.

When creating a course, such as one that might help this example author, it is best to break the subject matter down into smaller, individual courses rather than attempt to create one epic course covering a plethora of topics. This allows students to concentrate on subjects specific to their immediate needs.

To craft a course with a measurable outcome for your students, start by envisioning the ultimate goal. What do you want your students to achieve by the end of the course? With a clear vision in mind, you can define your course objectives. Ensure that each objective is Specific, Measurable, Achievable, Relevant, and Time-Bound (SMART). These objectives will serve as the foundation for the entire course and provide students with a roadmap to success.

Armed with your learning objectives, you can design engaging content that captivates your students' attention. Leverage a variety of multimedia tools and resources, including videos, interactive quizzes, readings, and discussions (via Zoom, email, or course communities) to cater to different learning styles and preferences.

Understand the importance of each student's ability to measure their progress. Design a range of assessments that are aligned with your course objectives. These assessments not only allow the student to evaluate their learning progress but also reinforce key concepts and skills.

Throughout the course, make it a priority to provide timely and constructive feedback to students. Whether this is through personalized comments on assignments or virtual office hours for group or individual coaching, ensure that students receive the support they need to succeed. This feedback helps students track their progress and identify areas that need further improvement.

As the course progresses, offer incentives and rewards for accomplishment. This may take the form of recognition in the course community group, timely emails or voicemail messages congratulating the students for milestones achieved, or surprise bonuses released at specific points in the course. Some or all of these incentives and rewards can be automated.

Let's create a hypothetical course outline and assessment, examine the technology needed for online delivery, and consider how the course might be marketed.

Our hypothetical course title is A Practical Guide to Crafting Compelling Character Arcs.

Course Description

This online course provides fiction writers with the essential tools and techniques to create dynamic and engaging character arcs that resonate with readers. Through a combination of video lectures, exercises, and real-world examples, students will learn how to develop multidimensional characters that undergo meaningful transformation throughout a story. From defining clear character goals to mapping out the stages of change, this course equips writers with the skills needed to craft unforgettable character journeys.

Course Duration: six weeks (with approximately three to five hours of study per week)

Target Audience:

- Aspiring writers interested in improving their storytelling skills.
- Fiction authors who want to create more compelling and nuanced characters.
- Screenwriters who are seeking to develop engaging character arcs for film and television.

Prerequisites:

- Basic understanding of storytelling concepts.
- Familiarity with the three-act structure is helpful but not required.

Course Learning Objectives

Understanding the Fundamentals of Character Arcs:

- Define the concept of a character arc.
- Identify the key elements of a compelling character arc.
- Analyze examples from literature and film to illustrate different types of character arcs.

Creating Well-Defined Characters:

- Establish clear goals, motivations, and conflicts for your characters.
- Develop complex and relatable personalities through backstory and psychology.
- Utilize character questionnaires and exercises to flesh out characters.

Exploring Different Types of Character Arcs:

- Examine positive change arcs, negative change arcs, and flat arcs.
- Identify when each type of arc is appropriate for different storytelling purposes.
- Evaluate examples to understand the nuances of each type of arc.

Structuring Character Arcs Effectively:

- Understand the three-act structure and its relationship to character development.
- Map out the stages of character change, including the setup, progression, and resolution.
- Utilize plotting techniques such as the "character arc graph" to visualize character growth.

Crafting Compelling Transformation Moments:

- Identify pivotal moments that drive character development.
- Create internal and external conflicts that challenge characters to change.
- Explore techniques for depicting emotional and psychological growth.

Refining Character Arcs Through Revision:

- Develop strategies for revising and fine-tuning character arcs.
- Solicit feedback from peers and mentors to strengthen character development.
- Utilize revision checklists and techniques to ensure consistency and coherence in character arcs.

Assessment Methods

Character Development Exercises: Students will complete exercises throughout the course to develop and refine their characters' arcs. These exercises may include creating character profiles, outlining pivotal scenes, and analyzing character motivations.

Character Arc Analysis: Students will analyze examples of character arcs from literature and film to identify the key components of each arc. They will demonstrate their understanding of different types of arcs and their effectiveness in storytelling.

Character Arc Outline: Students will create a detailed outline of a character arc for a fictional character of their own creation. The outline will include key stages of change, pivotal moments, and character goals, motivations, and conflicts.

Peer Feedback and Revision: Students will provide feedback on each other's character arc outlines and revise their own outlines based on peer feedback. This process will allow students to apply course concepts and refine their understanding of character arcs.

Required Technology

Internet Connection: Students will need a stable internet connection to access the online learning platform, stream video lectures, participate in discussions, and submit assignments.

Computer or Mobile Device: Students can access the course materials and lectures using a computer, laptop, tablet, or smartphone. The online learning platform should be compatible with various devices and operating systems (define this per platform requirements).

Video Player: Students will need a device with a video player (e.g., YouTube, Vimeo) to watch prerecorded video lectures. Most modern web browsers come with built-in video players, but students may also need to download additional software or apps if required.

Word Processing Software: Students will need access to word processing software (e.g., Microsoft Word, Google

Docs) to complete written assignments and exercises. These documents can then be uploaded to the online learning platform for submission.

Webcam and Microphone (Optional): While not mandatory, students may benefit from having a webcam and microphone for virtual meetings, live Q&A sessions, or video presentations. This equipment enables more interactive and engaging communication with instructors and peers.

Delivery Method

Online Learning Platform: The course can be delivered through an online learning platform such as Thinkific, Teachable, or Pubfunnels. This platform will serve as the central hub for accessing course materials, lectures, assignments, and discussions.

Lecture Videos: The main content of the course, including lectures on character arc fundamentals, examples, and explanations of various techniques, will be delivered through prerecorded video lectures. These videos can be uploaded to the online learning platform for students to watch at their convenience.

Written Materials: Supplementary reading materials, such as articles, excerpts from books, and worksheets, will be provided as downloadable PDFs or web links on the online platform. These materials will reinforce key concepts covered in the video lectures and provide additional resources for further exploration.

Interactive Exercises: Students will engage in interactive

exercises, quizzes, and activities designed to develop their understanding and application of character arcs. These exercises can include character profile templates, brainstorming prompts, and scenario analysis.

Discussion Forums: Online discussion forums will be set up on the learning platform to facilitate interaction and collaboration among students. They can ask questions, share insights, and provide feedback to their peers on assignments and exercises.

Assignment Submission: Students will submit their assignments, such as character arc outlines and analyses, through the online learning platform. Assignments can be submitted as written documents, audio recordings, or video presentations, depending on the instructor's preferences.

Promotional Marketing

To effectively market the course, A Practical Guide to Crafting Compelling Character Arcs, it's essential to target aspiring writers, fiction authors, and screenwriters who are seeking to enhance their storytelling skills. Implement a combination of marketing strategies for a wider reach to writers and storytellers worldwide. The following are some marketing ideas to promote the course.

Content Marketing: Create a series of blog posts or articles on topics related to character development, storytelling techniques, and the importance of character arcs in fiction writing. You can share these articles on writing-focused websites, forums, and social media platforms.

Develop engaging content such as infographics, videos, or podcasts that highlight the course's value and provide tips and insights into crafting compelling character arcs. Share this content on relevant platforms frequented by writers and creatives.

Create high-quality, informative content that addresses common questions, challenges, and interests of your target audience. Publish regularly to demonstrate expertise, build authority, and attract inbound links from other reputable websites.

Social Media Campaigns: Launch targeted social media campaigns on platforms like Facebook, Instagram, X (formerly Twitter), and LinkedIn to reach writers and aspiring authors. Using eye-catching visuals, compelling copy, and relevant hashtags will attract attention and drive engagement.

Leverage social media advertising to target specific demographics, interests, and professions related to writing and storytelling. Experiment with different ad formats, including carousel ads, video ads, and lead generation ads, to maximize reach and conversions.

Email Marketing: Build an email list of subscribers interested in writing, fiction, and storytelling. Create a series of automated email sequences that introduce the course, highlight its key benefits, and provide testimonials or success stories from past students.

Optionally, offer exclusive discounts, early bird pricing, or bonuses to subscribers who enroll in the course or refer others to join. Expand your reach by encouraging recipients to share the offer with their networks.

Partnerships and Collaborations: Partner with writing organizations, author communities, literary magazines, and writing conferences to promote the course to their members and followers. Offer to guest post on their blogs, participate in webinars or panel discussions, or provide exclusive discounts for their members.

Collaborate with influential authors, writing coaches, or industry experts who can endorse the course and share it with their audience. Consider offering them complimentary access to the course in exchange for promotion or testimonials. You might even consider offering an affiliate program that compensates them for paying students.

Webinars and Workshops: Host free webinars or workshops on topics related to character development and storytelling to provide upfront value and generate interest in the course. Use these events to highlight your expertise, preview course content, and interact with potential students.

Collect email addresses from the webinar attendees and follow up with targeted offers or invitations to join the full course. To incentivize action, provide attendees with special discounts or bonuses for enrolling within a limited time.

Search Engine Optimization (SEO): Optimize your website, blog, and course landing pages with relevant keywords, meta tags, and descriptions to improve visibility in search engine results. Focus on long-tail keywords related to writing, character arcs, and storytelling to attract organic traffic from individuals actively seeking writing resources.

Remember, creating an online course is a multifaceted endeavor that requires careful planning, effective communication, and a deep understanding of both subject matter and audience needs. Craft your courses with measurable outcomes and provide the resources your students need to succeed.

———————

Paula Judith Johnson is an award-winning author and hostess of the Writing Romance Mastery Summit. Get Paula Judith Johnson's <u>Seductive Storylines Checklist</u>.

CREATING A SUCCESSFUL COURSE
BY CAROL L. MONSON DO. MS

Life is a journey from birth to death—hopefully with a lot of good and happy times in between. My journey has taken me many places in life. I am a physician, a professor, a psychotherapist, and most recently a nonfiction author. And, as a professor in a medical school, I have written many online courses.

Success does not come by accident or luck; it is usually the result of planning and hard work. It begins with defining your goals and not letting others define them for you. Success is elusive because it is different for everyone. When you decide to be successful, you must devise a strategy. Ask yourself this question: Is it necessary for others to see you as successful, or is it essential that you *feel* successful?

Staying positive while you pursue success is a must because life is better when you feel positive. Along the way, you will enjoy your work because you have chosen it. You become motivated, focused, and passionate, and therefore, you will have fun on this journey. Becoming successful involves risk-taking and sometimes results in mistakes, but you benefit because you are pushed to learn self-reliance, self-confidence, and resilience.

The most important thing I have learned throughout my life is that no matter how much you know, no matter how hard you work and how much you try, you can never please everyone. There will always be people who don't like what you do, how you do it, or who you are. Some days, it can feel like you can't please anyone. I can guarantee that you will experience these feelings and have days like that as you plan and create your courses and pursue your success.

Early in my first career as a psychotherapist, I was tasked with creating a course that would train others to deliver mental health services. I was employed by a state agency whose mission was to innovate the delivery of adult psychiatric care to our state's population. My assignment involved consulting with a county mental health center in a small city surrounded by a rural area. My first task was to become familiar with the county we served, the people employed in the county center, and how current services were delivered. In course creation, that would be called defining my audience.

As I defined my audience, I spent at least one day per week in the county mental health center observing and working with their therapists to study how they delivered adult psychiatric care. I co-chaired group therapy sessions with them to demonstrate my clinical skills. This increased my credibility and demonstrated my expertise as a therapist. I also met regularly with the administrator and the medical director. This increased my knowledge of their treatment philosophies and roles in the center's care delivery. I shared information about our agency and the innovative changes in the state mental health code. We had discussions about how acute mental health care had changed in our state and how we might work together. The result would be to deliver better mental health care to our mutual clients. I shared my plans of developing a course for staff training and requested their help and cooperation. This equates with defining the purpose of your course and objectives for your students to learn, as well as making sure to interact with your audience.

Several days per week, I, along with another staff member, visited with clients previously hospitalized in our facility and now residing in this county. These clients' acute problems were improved, and they transitioned into local community placements. We met with them regularly to verify that their recurring problems were under control and being managed. We shared this responsibility jointly with the county mental health center. What we did and how we did it would be described in detail in several training modules. Each module in my topic list would have a description of our educational objectives and the expected outcomes after completing this course. In your course creation, this defines what can be expected and how it will be delivered.

Next, I added references from the current literature that

applied to my course content. This would further verify the techniques and methods I was teaching, giving the students confidence that my expertise was gained through studying the methods of experts and applying them. This step may or may not fully apply to your course creation, but it was needed in mine.

I then added exercises that allowed my learners to experience and practice the techniques that they were taught. Rehearsing skills before they are used builds confidence in the learner. There was a quiz at the end of each module that was self-scored, allowing the learner to assess their competency in that skill. If needed, they could return to review content material again. An evaluation was included at the end of the module to gain feedback, assess the difficulty of the content, and identify what else could have been included in the course. An ongoing evaluation helps the course creator keep the content growing and changing over time.

After successfully completing my course, the learners would then be directly supervised while they worked with our clients. They could practice their skills, increase their confidence, and assure themselves of their competency to work independently. This was needed in my course but may not be needed in yours unless you are offering a recognized credential.

Regular meetings with my supervisor and the medical director of our agency unit occurred to assess my progress on course content and construction. Both reviewed my course description and modules and provided constructive suggestions prior to launch. Their advice was incorporated into my course, which I then shared with the administrator of the county mental health center and requested her help with any changes. External review of your content prior to launch is recommended.

When my training course was released within our agency unit, I was excited to see my results. My course received excellent reviews from those completing the training, with a few minor changes suggested. Overall, my supervisor and medical director were pleased with the results, and I was happy my hard work paid off. This training course was then released for use in other agency units with similar positive results. Starting with a small group of people to beta test your course gives you the opportunity to get feedback and make corrections before you launch widely.

With growing confidence, I took copies of my training course to the county mental health administrator and medical director for implementation. The medical director liked the course, but the administrator, who was in charge of any changes in staff training, did not. I was stunned by her response, as her previous feedback had been positive. When asked what her objections were, she replied, "This may be fine for your fancy place up north, but we are going to do things here the way we have always done them. The help I gave you was for the benefit of your people's training, not mine." And with that, she said we were done. It was then I realized there would be nothing that I could say or do that would change her mind. My course was never going to please her, and I knew it.

It was a very hard lesson at that time in my life, and one I never forgot. Afterward, I spoke with my supervisor and our unit medical director. They reassured me that I had done everything I could, but told me that they could not convince her to change her mind. Their plans were to continue using my training course in other counties.

At the time, my life was changing in other ways. I was offered a job in another state at a higher salary, with better benefits and working conditions. I had less than a month to give my notice, find a place to live, pack my belongings, and move. I didn't think that the experience with this course entered into my decision to leave, but looking back, I am sure it affected my decision. My skin was thinner then, maybe because it was the first course I had written. It took a long time before I wrote another.

Later, as I matured and understood that I was my toughest critic, that changed. In my mind, even though I knew it was impossible to be perfect, I still tried to be. Back then, I overlooked all the positive comments, and focused on the one very negative comment my work received. Remember, no matter how much you know, no matter how hard you work and how much you try, you can never please everyone. I was successful then because I met my goals for success. I am more successful now because I survived that experience and learned from it.

There will always be people who will take your course, then leave you a scathing email or review, want their money back, or threaten to sue you. Get used to it. You can't please everyone; sometimes you can't please anyone. If you are honest and have done your best work, you can please yourself. Then at least one person is pleased, and you become successful because you have met your own goals.

Carol L. Monson, DO. MS. Is a psychotherapist, physician, author, and nationally known speaker. You may learn more about her at her website https://agingoptimally.org/.

6

LOVE YOUR KRYPTONITE
BY BARB GRANT

W hen I thought about launching my first course, I could feel my palms sweating. I swallowed hard and took a deep breath.

My situation was a little unique. I built and delivered online courses in large corporations for thirty years. But this was different. As John Wick would say, this was personal. My name, my course, my reputation.

I started my career as an e-learning consultant. In the nineties, I developed learning products for energy companies and telcos. Throughout my career, I have learned many things about developing and delivering successful online courses. I've seen what works and what doesn't.

Here are ten things you must do to create an incredible course:

1. Understand your target audience's needs.

2. Develop clear learning objectives.
3. Manage your time well.
4. Craft structured lessons.
5. Create engaging content.
6. Design for your users, *not* yourself.
7. Conduct rigorous quality assurance.
8. Adapt to the latest technology.
9. Communicate lessons effectively.
10. Market effectively.

However, mindset looms large over all these specific skills and actions. I was dead scared about putting my course out there. I was terrified that people wouldn't like it and that the course (and I) would fail. Being a Kiwi, a native of New Zealand, I also have a strong dislike of selling. It tends to be in our DNA. We like understated. Statements like, "Look at me," "Buy my course," and "My course is *so great*," don't square easily with our national values. I am the kind of person who will leave a store if a salesperson makes a beeline for me. That's if they have an obvious pushy demeanor. I hate selling. So, you have to find a way of selling your course that aligns with your values. It must feel authentic, or you won't be able to sustain it.

Therefore, this chapter's lesson is about learning to love your kryptonite. In other words, take a breath and embrace what you find hardest. But do it in small bites, and then do something you would love to return to tomorrow. You can't love all the kryptonite in one day. The other option is to outsource the bits you don't love and could be better at. But on a tight budget, and for your first product, that may not be an option. It wasn't for me.

The kryptonite I needed to learn to love the most was pricing and promoting. I'll focus on these two things in this chapter.

First, of course, you must decide you really *want* to do it. What is your why for becoming a digital course creator and marketer? Mine was so I could stop commuting by plane away from my family every week. I was sick of a fifty-plus-hour week in large corporate or public sector organizations. Knowing this worked well. When I doubted myself and my motivation waned, I pictured getting on another flight and unpacking in another faceless hotel room. The thought was highly motivating.

Next, I set myself an aggressive target. This is a way to end procrastination. It's best to embrace the "done is better than perfect" mindset. Frank Herbert tells us in *Dune* that "Fear is the mind-killer," but perfectionism isn't far behind it. I bought Pubfunnels in March of 2023 and decided my first course would launch in June of the same year. Yes, I gave myself three months. Then, I put it out there to my community on LinkedIn. I told them the course was coming and that it would teach the detailed "how-to" for the ideas outlined in my first book, which launched in March. Gulp. Putting it out on social media holds your feet to the fire. You don't want to have to rewind the promise. Doing this was definitely clutching my kryptonite.

And after that was pricing. It helps you to know your target price point for course development. The knowledge gives you guardrails for how much detail you want. You can get clarity on what topics to focus on and how long lessons should be. Then, you develop learning objectives calibrated to your agreed price point. These steps help you manage and meet buyer expectations.

Because the thought of charging people was a real struggle, I decided to take a softer approach. First, I worked out the core concepts I wanted to teach. Then, I advertised the course via LinkedIn, my website, and a landing page. I stated I would teach the first cohort in live sessions for a reduced price. This approach means you can co-design with your learners and guarantees that the content will be relevant to your audience.

I also focused hard on the course's value to get over my block about charging. If charging is an issue for you, think instead of all the people your course will help. The reframe is essential to shift your mindset.

In hindsight, I priced the introductory price too low. If I did it again, I would work harder to accept my teaching value and price it up. Sometimes, learning to value your *own* value is the hardest thing! Right now, I'm increasing the price. So far, I've priced it up twice. Incrementing is another good way to learn your market and the price it will bear.

Teaching the first cohort live had advantages. It took the pressure off providing fully developed content for launch. Instead, I worked out the key concepts. Then, I built a few slides with exercises. These provided structure for the discussion in the live coaching sessions but with the flexibility to test if my approach was on the right track. Live sessions are an excellent way to gather this proof of concept. Your learners will let you know what works and what doesn't.

The other point I would make here is that it's crucial to nail your course blueprint. This visual maps out the lessons in your course. You want to ensure the sequence is spot on and the lessons are broken down into manageable chunks. You should also build on the concepts taught in the early lessons in those that follow. Creating your content like this gives your course an excellent "shape." Throughout, be clear on the promise (what problem does your course solve?). Then, ensure it delivers neatly on that promise.

If pricing made my palms sweat a bit, the thought of promoting my course was enough to make me cry a river. You spend much time pouring your blood, sweat, and tears into building your course. But at that point, nobody knows about it. Like writing a book, you have to learn to put it out there and affirm that it will deliver on its promise. It's never too early to start promoting it. In fact, it is better to start this as soon as you have the idea for the course.

The traditional course marketing approach includes advertising, funnels, and webinars. It would be best to have a strategy to promote and sell that works for you. I chose a webinar to launch and used a racy meme relating to my subject matter to promote it on social media. The meme featured Pedro Pascal wearing a red Valentino coat. I added a sassy tagline about my profession of business change management. This approach almost doubled my email list size and ensured I had a great audience for my webinar.

Remember that when you run webinars, you should expect a fraction of those who sign up to show up. My attendance rate was 45 percent of sign-ups, which is high!

The next hurdle was designing and launching the email sequence for the webinar. I realized this was more of my kryptonite. I've bought many digital courses in my time but paid little attention to the timing, sequence, or content. Now, I had reason to become very interested. I hired an ex-colleague, who had become a support partner for a significant learning platform. They helped me craft the email sequence. This gave me the confidence to love my kryptonite and do the work myself. But it also assured me I was doing the right things.

I had a great turnout at the webinar and sold the course to an enthusiastic first cohort. But, I decided to change the format slightly for the next webinars. Usually, you extensively introduce what you're teaching in the webinar. Then, you present your credentials to teach it. Then, you do a piece on how great your product is. Videos like this on YouTube have me shouting at the screen, "Get on with it!" In my next webinar, I will diverge from this standard playbook and make the introductory section shorter. I decided to change something else as well. In the first webinar, I had included an actionable fifteen-minute exercise. The exercise was the taster for the course content. An exercise is recommended because people experience the value *before* getting to the webinar's selling section. As this creates more desire to buy, I will make the exercise longer and more interactive.

In my profession, many people talk about the theory of

change. I concentrate on how to deliver it. Focusing on the actionable is my major point of difference. I help change agents get practical runs on the board. Similarly, you want to be laser-focused on the problem you solve. Also, how is your solution better than that of competitors? Flesh out in detail how your buyers will know you solved their problem. In our amazing technical age, we have great tools like ChatGPT-4 to help create excellent sales copy. Ask the AI to use sales copy models like AIDA (Attention, Interest, Desire, and Action) to build your sales content.

But back to kryptonite. You need to love your kryptonite, a.k.a. things that repel you, and then take a break to do other things you love. In my case, this was working on branded course materials in Canva. If you like aesthetics and are creative (which you are if you're developing a course), then Canva is your friend. It's an intuitive application that gives so much scope for self-expression. Your audience engagement and comprehension will be higher if your course looks good. Aesthetics matter for effective teaching, so use lots of visual storytelling. A few well-chosen pictures to prompt a learner's understanding trump a thousand words. Your stories will stick most with your learners long after they complete the course.

Like most things, you grow into the unknown and then regroup. Rest, take a breath, go again. And that's the pattern you need to follow: wind up, unwind and regroup, go again, rest and regroup, and so on.

There's still plenty of growth in my future as I plan my next webinar and decide on the promotional strategy. Plus, I am planning my second course. But growth is opportunity. Loving your kryptonite is how you grow and improve at your work. Are you ready to love your kryptonite? Then, let's get to it!

Barb Grant is a business change management consultant, opera singer, and author. Her first book, Change Management That Sticks, was an Amazon #1 bestseller and won gold in the Organizational Design category of the 2023 Global Book Awards. Her second book is about actionable strategies to manage health and is inspired by her own story as someone living with chronic pain. Find out more about Barb and what she does at www.barbgrant.com

7

CRAFTING A SUCCESSFUL LEARNING EXPERIENCE

BY J.K. WINN

Embarking on the journey of creating a compelling course is akin to crafting a compelling story. Just as a writer relies on story structure as the foundation of their narrative, course creators must adhere to a set of principles and guidelines to ensure the success of their educational endeavors. In this exploration of "The Course Creator's Code," we delve into the essential elements necessary for crafting a successful learning experience.

Understanding the Framework

Much like a writer must grasp the intricacies of story structure to craft a captivating narrative, course creators must understand the framework of course development. The foundation of any successful course lies in its structure, which provides learners with a clear roadmap to navigate the learning journey. By embracing the classic structure, creators can organize their course content in a logical sequence, ensuring a cohesive and engaging learning experience.

Creating a course involves a meticulous process of planning, organization, and execution. Creators must carefully design the structure of their course, considering factors such as learning objectives, target audience, and instructional design principles. Outlining the key components of each act —introduction, development, and conclusion—allows creators to provide learners with a coherent framework for understanding and assimilating course content.

Building Suspense and Engagement

Just as suspense propels a story forward, engagement is essential in capturing and maintaining learners' interest throughout the course. Creators must infuse their course with elements that foster curiosity, intrigue, and active participation. From interactive quizzes and assignments to multimedia content and discussions, every component should serve to immerse learners in the subject matter, driving their motivation to learn and explore further.

Engagement is not merely about presenting information; it's about creating meaningful interactions that stimulate curiosity and critical thinking skills. Creators can leverage various instructional strategies, such as gamification, case studies, and peer collaboration, to foster active engagement and participation. By incorporating interactive elements that encourage exploration and discovery, creators can create a dynamic learning environment that captivates learners' attention and promotes deeper learning.

Creating a Rich Learning Environment

Like the setting in a story, the learning environment plays a crucial role in shaping the overall experience for learners. Whether it's through vivid descriptions, immersive multimedia, or real-world examples, a rich and dynamic setting is important to enhance the learning process. Incorporating elements that resonate with learners' interests and experiences will create a sense of belonging and relevance, fostering deeper engagement and retention of knowledge.

A rich learning environment goes beyond aesthetics; it encompasses the entire ecosystem of the course, including instructional design, technology infrastructure, and support resources. The platform must be user-friendly, accessible, and conducive to active learning. By providing learners with a seamless and immersive learning experience, creators can enhance their motivation, satisfaction, and overall learning outcomes.

Developing Dynamic Learning Milieu

In the world of online learning, learners are the protagonists of their own educational journey. Creators must hook their audience—in this case, learners—by understanding their motivations, aspirations, and challenges. By acknowledging the diversity of learners' backgrounds, learning styles, and preferences, course content can be tailored to meet the needs of individuals, fostering a more personalized and impactful learning experience.

Course development is about more than just providing information; it's about creating meaningful connections and empathy between learners and content. Creators can employ storytelling techniques, such as case studies, testimonials, and role-playing scenarios, to bring concepts to life and make them relatable to learners' experiences. By highlighting the relevance and applicability of content to learners' goals and aspirations, creators can foster a sense of ownership and investment in the learning process.

Navigating Conflict and Resolution

Just as characters in a story confront obstacles and challenges, learners must navigate through conflicts and complexities in their journey. Creators must anticipate potential roadblocks and provide learners with the tools, resources, and support they need to overcome them. Whether it's through interactive tutorials, peer collaboration, or personalized feedback, it's important to empower learners to persevere through challenges and achieve their goals.

Conflict and resolution are integral components of the learning process, providing learners with opportunities for growth, reflection, and self-discovery. Learning activities that simulate real-world challenges and dilemmas allow learners to apply course concepts in context and develop problem-solving skills. By guiding learners through this process, creators can cultivate resilience, adaptability, and critical thinking skills that are essential for success in today's complex and dynamic world.

Embracing Continual Growth

The journey of creating an online course is not static; it's a continual process of growth and evolution. Creators must embrace a mindset of continuous improvement, seeking feedback from learners, evaluating course effectiveness, and updating content to reflect emerging trends and best practices. Staying agile and adaptable will mean creators can ensure that their courses remain relevant, engaging, and impactful in an ever-changing educational landscape.

Continual growth requires creators to adopt a learner-centric approach to course development, prioritizing learners' needs, preferences, and feedback. Creators must actively solicit feedback from learners through surveys, assessments, and discussion forums, and use this feedback to inform iterative improvements to the course. Incorporating new technologies, pedagogical strategies, and learning resources will enhance the quality, accessibility, and effectiveness of courses over time.

Upholding Integrity and Ethics

Above all, creators must uphold the principles of integrity and ethics in their educational endeavors. Just as writers strive for authenticity and honesty in their storytelling, course creators must ensure the accuracy, objectivity, and inclusivity of their content. And fostering a culture of trust, respect, and transparency will cultivate a supportive learning community where learners feel empowered to explore, question, and grow.

Integrity and ethics are foundational principles that guide every aspect of course creation, from content development and delivery to assessment and evaluation. Creators must adhere to high standards of academic rigor, intellectual honesty, and fairness, ensuring that course content is accurate, balanced, and free from bias or discrimination. Promoting open dialogue, constructive feedback, and mutual respect will foster a culture of academic integrity and ethical conduct that upholds the values of scholarship and learning.

In essence, "The Course Creator's Code" serves as a guiding light for crafting a successful online learning experience. By embracing the principles of structure, engagement, authenticity, and continual growth, creators can unlock the true potential of online education, empowering learners to embark on a transformative journey of discovery and growth.

If you wish to read more of my stories, visit my website at jkwinn.com.

8

TARGETING SUCCESS: CRAFTING YOUR ONLINE COURSE FOR MAXIMUM IMPACT

BY MICHELE L. WHETZEL

When creating my first online course, I wanted it to appeal to as many people as possible. I held the common misconception that the broader the appeal, the greater the potential income. I figured the more students I could attract, the more income the course would produce. Following that logic, I believed that if I could make the course all things for all people, that would mean every person would be a potential client.

After spending months putting together my course, trying to throw as much information as possible into it, the feedback I received when I sent it to some beta testers was not at all positive. Here I thought I was providing a great value by including everything but the kitchen sink. It turns out, people are looking for solutions to their problems that are presented in a way they can easily implement them. They have been trying other solutions unsuccessfully, so they are looking for something new, the magic bullet that will make everything better. A course aiming to be everything to everyone can end up being nothing to anyone.

Discover Your Target Audience

The pivotal lesson I learned? Success in creating an online course hinges on being able to pinpoint your target audience and tailor the content to be attractive to as many people as possible within that audience. Rather than cast a wide net, focus on who you aim to serve.

It is important that you narrow down the ideal candidates for your course. Are they young, old, or somewhere in between? Male or female? Do they have some experience in this field, or are they brand new to it? Brainstorm other ways to narrow down your target audience.

Then create the course as if aiming at a specific person within that group. Try to understand their pain points, aspirations, and desires. Your course should feel like a personalized solution crafted specifically for them. The more a potential student believes you are speaking directly to them and their needs, the more attraction the course will gain.

Instead of worrying about losing potential students, be purposeful about narrowing the focus to aim directly at your target. Conduct research to identify the specific challenges your potential audience faces that you can help solve. It is more important to be the hero for your target audience member than to try to appeal to those on the fringes who will most likely not appreciate your offerings anyway.

Define Your Unique Proposition

Standing out in a crowded digital landscape requires carving your own niche. Create a course that presents the information and ideas in a unique way, and showcase its distinctive value proposition. There may be other similar courses out there, but you want your course to be in a lane of its own.

Analyze your would-be competitors' offerings and how they are presenting them. Look for gaps and opportunities for improvement, and add your own unique perspective, experiences, and insights to create a new and better course.

Crafting compelling content involves more than just delivering information. Adding storytelling about your experiences (or those of others), near-misses, and successes will engage your audience. Weave narratives, analogies, and metaphors throughout your course to make concepts relatable. Put together the overall theme of the material you will present, and start with a clear outline. Infuse each step with your own personal touches and wisdom gained through your experiences.

Embrace Learning Diversity

When creating a course, it is important to keep in mind that everyone learns differently. Try to cater to as many learning styles as possible so the maximum number of people taking your course will come away having gained the knowledge you are sharing. You may want to conduct early surveys or assessments to determine learning preferences. By catering to these preferences, you can create a more inclusive and effective learning experience.

Think about including some of the styles below or a combination of them. Listed with each learning style are the types of materials you can provide to help learners assimilate the information best:

1 **Visual Learners** – slides, diagrams, infographics, animations, demonstrations, videos, real-life examples, color coding and other visual cues.

2 **Auditory Learners** – narrated presentations, podcasts, recorded lectures or interviews, verbal discussions or debates in forums or live sessions, added sound effects or music for emphasis.

3 **Read/Write Learners** – provide lecture notes, transcripts, ebooks, articles, research papers, or case studies that are related; ask students to do writing exercises, summaries, reflections.

4 **Kinesthetic Learners** – hands-on activities, simulations, case studies, interactive exercises where students can apply concepts in practical ways; opportunities for movement during learning like pacing while listening to lectures or using physical props for demonstrations.

5 **Interactive Learners** – quizzes, polls, simulations, games, role-playing activities, discussion boards, collaboration, peer-to-peer learning, group projects, or other interac-

tive exercises that encourage hands-on practice and application.

6 Sequential/Linear Learners – content provided in logical, step-by-step manner with clear outlines, structured modules, and organized course materials; progress-tracking tools to help them navigate through the course content systematically.

7 Global/Holistic Learners – big-picture overviews, concept maps, mind maps, interdisciplinary connections to help learners see the larger context and relationship between topics; encourage critical thinking and synthesis of information.

By incorporating a diverse range of instructional methods and materials, you can create a more inclusive learning environment that caters to the needs of various learning styles. When you offer flexibility and options for how learners engage with the content, it can further enhance their learning experience.

While you can't cater to every learning style in a single course, you can aim to offer a balanced mix of materials to appeal to a broad audience. For example, for my course I decided to create five video modules as the main vehicle for presenting the information, but I also provide supporting written materials with examples of how to create certain types of documents, as well as links to specific websites to get more information.

Also, my course includes assessments learners need to fill in to be sure they are headed in the right direction. If someone is an audio learner, they can listen to the videos rather than watch them. The videos are numbered and present the steps in a logical sequence so learners can achieve the end goals quickly but in an orderly fashion. At the end of each video, there are action steps required for the students to implement and create.

Summary

I have found through personal experience that you need to find your target audience rather than try to be all things to all people. Once you have honed in on that group, create your course as if you were speaking to one specific person within that target group to help them solve their nagging problem. Since you are never sure how that person will best absorb the information they need to implement your solutions, provide various delivery method options.

When your target audience members believe you have a unique offering that speaks directly to them and their needs, you will not only attract dedicated followers but will also foster a community of learners eager for your next offering.

Michele Whetzel is a nonprofit expert and author of the bestselling book So, You Want to Start a Nonprofit, Now What? Visit her website at 501Guide.com

9

CREATING MINDSET SHIFTS THAT TRANSFORM

BY SALLY SAXON JD

Today, many people are hungry for breakthroughs in various aspects of their lives. They seek a new level of success, expertise, confidence, clarity, enthusiasm, or passion. Or perhaps a new level of inner peace, purpose, freedom, or understanding.

In one class I took several years ago, the teacher/trainer was talking about life purpose and asked several people what they did for a living. He then reframed their job or profession in different words that totally changed their perspective of their work.

I'll never forget his interaction with one student in particular. It created a life-changing and memorable experience for *me* even though I was not even the one he was working with! I don't remember much else about that entire event, but I will probably remember those few minutes for the rest of my life.

The woman he was working with described her job as an event planner. As the teacher delved a bit further into what kinds of tasks she actually did, he reframed her work as a "creator of magical moments." I'm not sure how that new "job description" impacted *her* in the long run, but it definitely had a lasting impact on *me*! It's like what they say about insurance salespeople: They're not really selling insurance—they're selling peace of mind.

The teacher was providing a life-changing experience that went beyond knowledge and understanding of the subject matter. It reframed the woman's identity and purpose.

We've all heard the expression that people may not remember anything you said, but they'll remember how you made them feel.

When I heard the teacher reframe the woman's job as a "creator of magical moments," it quickened something in me. It resonated with me because I realized in that moment that I, too, had the potential to be a "creator of magical moments." If I got nothing else out of that class, that one nugget was well worth the time and expense. It was priceless because the implications were huge.

Seeing your role as a course creator in terms of being a "creator of magical moments" can change the impact you have on students. That "job description" can apply to all kinds of work, especially course creators, because they are teachers, and teachers have a unique opportunity to create unforgettable and transformative moments or experiences in their students' lives.

Maybe there's a different moniker that resonates more with you than "creator of magical moments." Use whatever words you want, so long as they resonate and carry an emotional charge for you. Try to reframe the work you do with words that generate greater excitement for *you*.

When you think back to your years in school, was there at least one teacher who created a magical moment or transformative experience for you that impacted the course of your life? I had a few teachers in my school days like that, and several others later who helped me achieve a major breakthrough.

What did those teachers do that was so different than the others? For me, it was two things. One was how they made me feel about myself. They encouraged me and applauded my efforts and successes. They spoke to my potential and made me believe I was capable of achieving anything I set my mind to. They saw in me what I couldn't see in myself.

Second, they changed my mindset, which includes how I see my identity, my potential, and my value. They taught about limiting beliefs, how we sabotage ourselves, and the power we all have to change our results in any area of life by changing how we think.

Both of these elements, emotional impact and mindset, can be applied to teaching about practically any subject matter. They also enhance your students' consumption of your course content, no matter what the subject is. The "magical moments" example above actually involved both elements at the same time. That's probably why it was so impactful for me.

Does thinking about yourself as a "creator of magical moments" (or other moniker with an emotional charge) shift your perspective of yourself as a course creator? Does it give you new ideas as to how you might design your course?

Are any of your students having trouble finishing your course, or unknowingly sabotaging their own success? Even if they know your course content very well, are they having difficulty getting the results they want?

The Power of Emotional Impact

A big part of the process of transformation involves emotion. One of the best and easiest ways to change one's thinking and facilitate a breakthrough is through an experience that has a strong emotional impact. It has to do with how the brain works, how new neural connections are made and strengthened until they become imprinted in your subconscious mind.

The greater an emotional impact you can create, the quicker transformation happens. So think for a few moments, and let your imagination run wild: In light of your course content, what could you do to create a powerful emotional impact that creates a mindset shift for your students?

The Power of a Mindset Lesson or Module

Regardless of the subject matter of your course, one way you can help your students experience a transformational breakthrough or a magical moment is by incorporating a lesson or module on mindset. For some course creators, that may be the whole subject of their course! If that's you, then think of new ways to create that emotional charge and a shift in how your students see themselves and the true purpose of their work.

Our external results are a reflection of our internal beliefs. So if we want different results, we have to change the seeds of thought and belief that are producing those results.

For those whose course subject matter is not all about mindset and changing how we think, consider including a mini-teaching on mindset and the power your students have to plant and grow different kinds of "thought seeds" that produce the results they want.

It's not enough for students to have knowledge or expertise in the subject matter of your course. Limiting beliefs about their ability to succeed in applying what they learned from you can sabotage results. But knowing how the brain works and how to "program" it to get the results we want is both fascinating and indispensable if we want to create the greatest impact.

I've taken courses, such as real estate investing, where a key session was all about mindset issues. The teacher knew that the main reason why many students fail at real estate investing was not because they didn't know the investing strategies or the mechanics of how to do certain kinds of deals. The problem was their mindset—limiting beliefs that they didn't even realize were sabotaging their results.

Including a mindset component in your course can help to create breakthroughs and magical moments to enhance your students' experience and their likelihood of completing your course and telling others about it.

Using Stories and Examples to Create a Mindset Shift

Stories and case studies are great for helping students understand concepts and be encouraged by real-life examples.

I've taught a class entitled, "Astound Yourself." It's based on the Thomas Edison quote, "If we did all the things we're capable of, we would literally astound ourselves!"

I share my story of going from not being able to walk more than fifty to one hundred yards at a time in my late fifties because of extreme pain of an arthritic joint in one foot, to completing over one hundred half marathons and ten full marathons in six years' time in my sixties!

I use that story to encourage my students that much more is possible for them than they think they can do, achieve, overcome, or change. It stirs their attention and makes them curious to find out how I did that.

A story can also enhance your credibility in the students' eyes. If it shows how you overcame a big problem or reveals your willingness to be vulnerable, or if you did or achieved something that seemed impossible, that helps to build the "know, like, and trust" factors.

A story doesn't even have to be your own. It can be someone else's experience. Case studies are great examples.

You could even use very short videos or clips to illustrate a point.

It's great to include examples of how other students of yours were able to achieve their breakthroughs and transformation based on your training or teaching. If you're just getting started and don't yet have testimonials like that to share, you could offer a few people a chance to go through your course for free in exchange for a testimonial of the impact they experienced.

Engagement and Interaction

How many ways can you think of to engage your students and encourage them to take steps toward their ultimate goal? We all know some of the common ways to do that, such as question-and-answer sessions, games, and "hot seats" where you focus on one student at a time and brainstorm their situation. I've seen many people, including myself, experience a transformation in Q & A and "hot seat" sessions.

But what about other kinds of exercises or activities, such as those that build confidence or help to overcome fears?

Some leadership training courses offer great ideas that can be applied in other types of courses as well. I went through a leadership training course once that involved a "ropes" course. It forced us to confront our fears and perceived limitations in several news ways. We broke some boxes symbolizing limiting beliefs. We climbed and then jumped off of tall poles (harnessed in, of course!). We had to lean way over the edge of a steep cliff (harnessed in again), and also had to figure out how to get the entire class up and over a twelve-foot wooden wall without any ladders or other props. It looked impossible, and it was scary, but we did it!

There are plenty of other kinds of interactive leadership training activities that can be done indoors and are not as physical. But their lessons are not limited in application to courses about leadership.

Creating memorable experiences often involves challenging people to do things they didn't think they could do. Don't hesitate to challenge your students in that way. It's like working out in the gym. You have to push yourself a little bit beyond what you can already comfortably do. Give students a challenge and opportunity to rise to the occasion. Prepare them in ways that build the belief that they can actually do new things they didn't think were possible.

What kind of experience could you create that would be so impactful that it would lead your students to tell others about it without you even asking them to do that? Not to mention that it will motivate them to want to come back for anything else you offer.

My hope for you is that, by implementing some of the suggestions in this chapter, your students will give you one of the biggest compliments you could ever receive: "Any class you teach, I want to take." If they say that, it's probably not just because your subject matter was excellent. Undoubtedly, it was also because of how you made them feel and shifted their mindset about what was really possible.

Sally Saxon is an award-winning and best-selling author of The COVID-19 Vaccines & Beyond . . . What the Medical Industrial Complex is NOT Telling Us; a speaker, podcast host and mentor. She can be reached through https://SallySaxon.com.

10

THE HERO'S JOURNEY
BY BERT A. AMSING

"I 'm the Map! I'm the Map! I'm the Map! I'm the Map!"

Now tell me the truth. Don't be shy. You actually sang those words to yourself as you read them, didn't you? Any parent with small children knows about Dora the Explorer and her sidekick, the Map. Whenever Dora has to solve a problem, she goes on a journey, and who better to help her get to her destination than her friend, the Map!

If you don't like Dora, we could talk about Dorothy and the yellow brick road. "We're off to see the Wizard. The Wonderful Wizard of Oz!" Dorothy wants to get back home, and the Wizard will know the way back. The yellow brick road is (conveniently) right in front of her, and all she has to do is follow it. There will be challenges and barriers, but there will also be new friends along the way (the Scarecrow, the Lion, and the Tin Man).

It isn't just children's stories and movies that follow this theme. Almost every great book of fiction is a variation on the hero's journey. A problem is encountered that must be overcome at great cost to our hero (or heroine). The first step is to accept the challenge and begin the journey either alone or in the company of others (think Frodo and his companions). But they need a plan, a map, a yellow brick road to follow. They need someone along the way who can guide them past the barriers they will face (think Gollum) and help them get to the journey's end.

This hero's journey isn't just for fiction; it also applies to nonfiction. After all, we are all called to accomplish great things, to change, to grow, to become the best versions of ourselves that we can be, and that is also a journey fit for a hero.

If you are overweight and diabetic, your "call to action" may be to lose fifty pounds, learn to eat a healthier diet, and exercise more. Not so easy. You have a lifetime of bad habits holding you back. The hero within you will have to take hold of the problem and pay the price to solve it. Yes, you are a hero, not just because of your sacrifice but because you do it for the ones who love you.

If you are struggling to get ahead financially and are caught in the trap of poverty, you may feel the call to make money online and change your financial destiny. The hero within you will have to make some changes, learn to be resilient, and find the resources needed for the journey. Information is important. Transformation is vital.

If you have an important relationship that has been broken and you want to restore it, you may feel called to learn to be a better version of yourself, find ways to forgive, or just communicate. You are on a journey, and it is a journey fit for heroes because you will encounter obstacles and barriers that must be overcome. There will be times when you will want to give up. There will be times when you lose the path. Do not lose heart. There is always help along the way.

And that is where we come in as course creators. We are the guides, the maps. We are the yellow brick road. We will show you the way to Mordor. We have been there, and we know what awaits you along that journey.

It's true, isn't it? You know the way. If not, you probably shouldn't be creating a course about it. You can start with the problem and show your reader the solution, but that isn't enough. Your personal experiences, the details of the journey, the problems that come up and how to solve them are vital to your job as the guide. Clarity is your currency.

Joseph Campbell, in 1949, wrote the book *The Hero with a Thousand Faces,* which identified common themes in mythological narratives. He came up with seventeen stages to the journey divided into three acts: departure, initiation, and return. Not every story has all the stages or even has them in the same order, but the hero's journey is still there. Although there is a plot and a setting, the focus is on the development of the hero.

What is surprising is that this "story" approach can be used for so many things other than a work of fiction. We are the "hero" of our own story. That isn't merely "marketing" but truth. We are on a journey through life. Change will be necessary. Barriers will come up. We will need a guide, a map, or a consultant. We will need products, information, and strategies.

In my case, I write about Christian spirituality. Another way to put it is to say that I write about life from the perspective of the Bible. I write both fiction and nonfiction, and you might say that it would be hard for me to incorporate this "esoteric" topic into the hero's journey. Quite the opposite, in fact. I doubt that there is a single topic out there that cannot be adapted to the hero's journey.

Take, for example, my book *Seeking Jerusalem: Discovering the Power of Spiritual Unity.* This is a work of nonfiction focused on the problem of broken relationships in the church, where there is often infighting and dissension among believers. The vision of a "New Jerusalem" is used in the Bible as the goal of the church. Seeking Jerusalem, then, is the journey toward that goal. It isn't a physical place but rather a description of how to live in the presence of God together as a church.

The problem is broken relationships within the church. The solution is to live in the presence of God together. So far so good. But we need more examples, more details, more meat on the bones. How do we get there? Does the Bible help us on this journey? Of course. The Bible is the map. The Holy Spirit is our guide. I am acting as the consultant who will interpret the information and put it in the context of our daily lives.

In fact, some people would say (including me) that the secret power of Christianity is the ability to heal broken relationships—first with God but then later with the people around us, including people in the church. If that is true, it gives people hope on this journey. Without hope (and faith) that there really is a solution and that we can find it and implement it, no one would embark on the journey.

This is the first step: the *Departure*. Part of that comes with being able to clearly define the problem. Some people claim that the more clarity you can bring to the problem, the shorter the journey will be. True. Part of it is also stating the solution clearly and making it believable, providing social proof that it works, and that it is reasonably attainable.

In the end, it isn't about the information that you teach them but about the transformation they need to go through. Your personal testimony to that transformation is key.

But now the journey has started, and your hero has decided to answer the call to action. This is where the fun begins. This stage is called *Initiation*. Now that our hero has left his ordinary world behind, he discovers a new world, new experiences, and new obstacles. A lot can happen here, but remember that this is about our hero. It isn't just about what is accomplished at the end of the journey but who he becomes along the way.

And that is certainly true in the church as well. There are stages to this journey of faith. We talk about confession, repentance, forgiveness, and reconciliation. This is nice-sounding "religious" language, but our job is to bring these concepts down to earth, explain them, and apply them in practical situations with lots of stories and examples.

Think of the barriers and obstacles associated with each

step the hero must take. *Confession* is about telling the truth and admitting your faults. Talk about dangerous. What if the person I confess to uses it against me? What if they make it public? What if they see me as weak and undeserving of their love? It's probably safer just to let sleeping dogs lie. Perhaps we should find an easier way to the Promised Land. The desert is simply too hot and uncomfortable. Asking the "what if" kinds of questions at each stage will generally uncover the obstacles and barriers that need to be overcome.

Look at the stage of *Repentance* (which means a complete turnaround or change). That's not so easy to do. I can't even stick to my diet, much less exercise three times a week. Change is hard for all of us, but that is because we try to do it on our own. New habits are best formed in the context of accountability to those who love us and appreciate our honest confession of weakness. Do you see how the stages are connected?

The secret sauce is the Biblical concept of *Forgiveness* based on the ministry and death of Christ on the cross. It is radically different from what most people understand about forgiveness. Getting this right is the key to everything else.

Reconciliation is just another name for a restored relationship with someone based on who they are as a "new creation" in Christ and not on who they are as a weak-willed, often-difficult human being. Each step of the way needs to be clearly defined and connected to each other so that you can guide the hero to the desired result.

And of course, there is the *Return,* where the hero comes

back to his familiar world a changed man. There is celebration, but there may also be other challenges since it usually involves changes in expectations, relationships, and the role of the hero in the community. We call it "living happily ever after," but some writers suggest that a whole new drama may unfold where the hero or heroine may, in fact, become the guide for others to follow in their footsteps. In the church, we call this role "the wounded healer."

What does all of this have to do with creating courses? Everything.

My particular process is to start with blogging, then create a book from those blog posts, and finally, create a course. When I blog, I have the hero's journey in mind to keep me on topic, but I also have to think about Google's ranking requirements for topical authority. That tends to be information-based, and they like posts with names such as, "The Ten Reasons Why Christians Don't Forgive Their Neighbors," which is not very helpful.

When I make a series of blog posts into a book, I tend to have more room for creativity. But even if the book is just a collection of blog posts, if you blog with the hero's journey in mind, you will be on the right track. But creating a great book from your blog posts is another journey for another day.

When it comes to making a course out of your book, blog, or post many people would suggest that you go from topical authority (teaching everything you know about a topic) to a cutting-edge strategy (teaching an effective way to do something). That is helpful but not enough. A focus on topical authority will largely be information-based. A focus on teaching a cutting-edge strategy is results-oriented. That isn't a bad thing; it just isn't enough.

A focus on the hero's journey will include your topical authority and will provide cutting-edge strategies to get the results that you promised, but you must put it in a context that is motivating and personal to your audience. You must go on the journey of transformation with them.

Bert A. Amsing is the author of Jesus Was an Alien (and Other Stories of Faith). He is also an international speaker and kingdom coach. You can reach him at info@bertamsing.com

11

SLAY THE DAY

BY SUE HUMPHREY

R ecently I decided to enter a new career. After over thirty years as a middle school teacher and administrator, I realized that retirement wasn't as rewarding as advertised. I needed more structure in my days. My actions during my working years had been governed by a school bell. A bell started and ended a class period, a bell woke me up each morning, a bell told me when to eat and even when I could go to the bathroom. Now I had no bells, no definite places to be other than doctor appointments. I knew I didn't want to continue this unstructured life.

I had funds saved and looked around to find what type of new opportunities were of interest. Since I had been coaching track-and-field for close to fifty years, I wanted to stay in the sports area. I had also studied journalism in school, so authoring a book and/or a course was on my bucket list. The more I researched current methods to share my experiences, it became evident that online programs were quickly becoming extremely popular. So, I eagerly investigated the idea of creating an online course.

The world had just gone through the pandemic of 2020, and we all were introduced to the world of virtual technology, especially in the field of education. Regardless of age, the citizens of the world discovered that to communicate with other human beings, we had to learn how to log in to a program called Zoom. We had to meet friends and new acquaintances through a screen. "You are still muted," became an exceedingly popular phrase in the English language.

We tried to teach others what buttons to push on our laptops to get better lighting, to change names on the screen tiles, and how to share screens.

Virtual coaching clinics and online courses occupied most of our time. Meeting new coaches and sharing training ideas online led to virtual coaching programs. Suddenly, a new world opened up to me!

After ten years of unstructured living, I realized I needed to become organized again and be much more productive for my mental and physical health. I was going to do this new project by developing online track-and-field coaching courses.

To enter this new world, I needed to revisit what habits helped me be successful in the past. I had a quick answer—I needed to develop and follow daily patterns. Previously, having routines had given my life structure and organization as I tackled my short-term and long-term goals. I desperately needed this structure again.

After taking a deep breath, I knew it was time to leave the carefree life of getting up whenever and floating from activity to activity. It was time to get my life back together. I was ready! I started the implementation of a morning routine and began to research my potential clients for an online course.

Every twenty-four hours, a new opportunity to achieve success began. Routines became easy to track once they were created and followed for a period of time. Scientists have studied the body's circadian cycle and discovered that our bodies function better when we establish a natural twenty-four-hour pattern. Our sleep cycles, hormone releases, and metabolism follow a twenty-four-hour cycle. Therefore, my plan of establishing a morning routine had scientific basis to it too.

Using this information, what steps was I going to take to create a plan toward successful course development? First, when my alarm shook me out of bed, I took a deep breath and a few moments to reflect on the opportunities I would be given that day. My first activity was to clearly reflect on the day's goals that I prepared the night before. I visualized myself successfully completing them, as they were the building blocks creating my vision. I listed five items that I had to do every morning. These items included doing diverse types of market research to see what problems my prospective students had and needed to solve. I also realized that developing a course outline catering to the needs of my clients was required for successful program development. Once these areas were completed, I continued to create the content for my course.

Journaling has been a popular method to record and organize our thoughts and feelings. Some people find that seeing the words and pictures that describe our thoughts really stabilizes them. This documentation helps our mental clarity and increases our overall productivity. When we feel positive about our daily accomplishments, our stresses are reduced during a challenging day. Marking off even small tasks can give us a sense of accomplishment. It's so rewarding to see a list of checked-off tasks at the end of a day!

It's quite easy to develop a timeline of tasks needed to develop and implement a course. The creation of a course is just a series of items to accomplish. Market research to discover the problem(s) of your potential client should be at the top of your to-do list. Once the problem to be solved has been identified, the steps that need to be completed should be listed.

Step by step, your project gets completed, and your "habit" leads to the development of your course.

Physical exercise of any type is also a vital component for a successful routine. Usually, I try to exercise early in the morning before the hectic events of the day crowd out my activities. Depending on your physical condition, you should plan out fifteen to twenty minutes with some type of activity to get your body's systems active after at least eight hours of sleep. There's really no excuse not to exercise with all the various apps or TV programs available to use. In addition, you can always go outside to run or walk.

To keep my creative juices flowing and my body refreshed, I drank a lot of water and made a nourishing drink or smoothie to drink while I studied and developed the various lessons for my online course.

Physical exercise also induces the release of endorphins. There are medical tests that show these endorphins lead to an improvement of a person's cognitive functions. When endorphins release in the body, these hormones improve mood and create a sense of well-being. This positive emotional state encourages a more open and flexible mind-set, which is crucial for creative thinking. When developing a new course in your niche, someone in a positive frame of mind should be willing to entertain unconventional ideas and take creative risks that lead to innovative and artistic expressions.

The release of endorphins can boost energy levels and improve mental clarity. With increased energy and focus, individuals can dedicate more sustained attention to creative tasks. For instance, an author might find themselves more energetic and focused after a run, allowing them to spend longer, more productive periods on course development.

Goal setting has been around for ages. If you're a morning person, it's good to prioritize the most important tasks on your to-do list. If you gain energy as the morning progresses, do some smaller tasks early and then conquer the major events later in the morning. Overall, successful completion of each item is the main goal. Different people have various methods of successfully working through their lists.

When developing an online course, it's vital that you develop your ideal plan, then revise steps as you work through the lessons with your clients and see how quickly you can mark off the steps leading to finalizing your course.

The exciting news is that as we repeatedly work on our routines and discover what works for us, these tasks begin to occur naturally. Research has shown that we'll feel fatigued or not as efficient if we don't follow our established rituals. Humans are creatures of habit, and when we develop routines and faithfully follow them, we develop patterns that hopefully lead us to productivity and healthier, happier lives.

The establishment of new routines might lead to excuses or reasons why you need to do something else. Telling yourself skipping one day won't matter starts a trail of failure. Dedication and overcoming doubt and various obstacles will be difficult at first, but completing the events on your list gets easier day by day, week by week, month by month. When your new routine becomes part of your behaviors, you should see positive results in all phases of your life.

An excellent resource is the book, *Atomic Habits*, by James Clear. He shares many reasons and examples of how and why habits are so important to overall success and happiness. Some of the concepts he addresses start with the creation of small habits, and then once they're mastered, he suggests adding a similar habit to extend the one already created. Again, this pathway is vital to a positive establishment of an online course/program.

As mentioned earlier, journaling plays a key role in building a routine that will help someone improve their life. Keeping track of one's progress and/or setbacks is invaluable to monitor success and identify areas for improvement. Journaling can extend into writing time if you're an author and/or developing a business. You can create a book and other products to go with your course.

Some famous authors claim that their best creative hours are before 7:00 a.m. Most homes or offices are quiet early in the morning, and distractions are at a minimum. If you can structure a routine to accomplish many of your more challenging tasks before midmorning, you'll feel more successful. Likewise, if you're an evening person, adjust your schedule accordingly. The main concept is to discover what routines work best for you and follow them.

In today's world of rewards and immediate satisfaction, it is important to provide structure leading to the creation of routines. Rewards can be intangible or tangible. Children or young people might want to receive a more concrete token at the beginning of habit creation. Adults or older young adults lean toward the satisfaction of seeing how routines help with structure and lead to more orderly lives. Improving our creativity and opening more opportunities should be motivation enough to keep following new patterns and even build upon them.

As we continue to pursue our dreams as course developers, we'll find that establishing a routine and set of behaviors will be the first steps taken toward this new goal. Success will be more likely to follow as you continue to create more routines and build new opportunities.

One of the most common excuses is, "I don't have time to add more to my day." My answer is, "How can you not do something to make your life more successful?" Business coaches stress that structure leads to results. When reading or listening to books written by successful people, a common thread throughout their stories is the creation of patterns or routines that they follow while working toward a goal.

How do you make this major shift in your thinking and behaviors? Can you continue when times are tough? What items should be part of your routine? All these questions race through your mind when deciding what changes to make and when to start. Realize that not every adjustment will have positive results right away. You will need to revise parts of your plan as you work toward your new schedule. Expect this part of the plan. Patience becomes a vital component of how we adjust and integrate new habits into our daily lifestyle. Every challenge begins with just one step, then the next, and the next, and the next, and so on.

Sue is a 3 time USA Olympic Track & Field Coach, author of "I Want To Run" and founder of the Gold Medal Coaches Summit series. You can get in touch with Sue at https:// suehumphreycoach.com/

12

TURN A COURSE INTO A BOOK
BY LINDA BERRY

Course First, Then Book

Have you given people you know consultations on a regular basis? Did you think of converting what you've been doing into a course, and then did? Apply this same concept and convert your course into a book!

The course you offer will dictate the type of book you will create. The best conversion to publication is that of nonfiction or memoir books which are either self-help or how-to, and sometimes both together.

There are many books in the market that are based on a course given by the author. For example, if you are presenting a series of business classes to entrepreneurs, you would create a how-to book in the field represented in your training.

Take a health and wellness program as an example: No

matter if it covers mental, physical or emotional well-being, this can be transformed into a successful self-help book. It's best to use case studies from clients who have successfully completed your program for this type of book.

Another viable option would be to write a how-to or self-help memoir. It is written just like a regular memoir, highlighting areas of your life to share with the reader, but the twist here is that you add something extra that will draw the reader into to your story. Make it more personal to them, and your life highlights become usable examples of what your course offers. What better way to show the reader that if you could do it, they can to.

The "teaching" memoir (as it's referred to) has become extremely popular over the past few years. It's also one that is easiest to create. All the research of the book is based on you and your experiences, focusing on a particular situation, hurdle or problem you had to overcome.

The material covered in this chapter explains the basics of transferring your course into a book format. Pay special attention to the TIP (Transfer Idea Process) portion after each section to get valuable guidance and resources to make the efforts to create your book the most effective.

Tip

Follow this outline to begin drafting your book based on the course you offer. Fill in as much information as you can on your first run through. You can always update, revise and change it later, especially after reading the following material. The main reason to complete this is to get your thoughts in order to start writing your manuscript.

Book Manuscript Outline

COVER: Use artwork from existing course promotion material

TITLE: Use course name in main title or subtitle

GENERAL FRONT MATTER PAGES:

- Copyright information and liability limits/disclaimer

- Dedication or acknowledgments

- Testimonials (satisfied course participants)

COURSE PROMOTION:

- Reader Call to Action (CTA) with Links

- Course * Training * Services * Products * Opt-In (Email List)

INTRODUCTION: Description of the course translated into what's covered in the book. Who would want to read this book and why it's important to know about this course. Emphasize the author who is also the course creator and administrator of the training being the expert on the topic covered.

BOOK CONTENTS: List of Chapters (10 to 12 total)

CHAPTER CONTENT:

- Lesson name part of chapter title

- Materials covered in the lessons and their importance in the overall course

- Client Case Studies

NOTE: Demonstrate what's covered in the training and

the success clients had during and after participating in the course. The readers relate themselves to these case studies, so using the CTAs (front and back of book) makes them contact the author to learn more and take the course.

-Recap of overall results from taking the lesson

-Lead-in to the next chapter and lesson covered

NOTE: May have to break one lesson material into two to three chapters depending on the length of the course.

GENERAL BACK MATTER PAGES:

AUTHOR BIO: Background, experience, and credentials (in third person)

COURSE PROMOTION: Reader CTA repeated (same as Front Matter)

REFERENCES OR REFERENCE GUIDE (if applicable)

GLOSSARY (if applicable)

Book Focus

It's very important to remember when preparing your outline that the book you are creating is an overview and explanation of what you teach, not a detailed description of what is taught in the entire course. Do not give away the farm!

Remember: less is more. You want people to get an idea of what you teach and how you do it—your style and approach. Show what makes you different from other trainers in the field. This way when they finish the book, they are excited to take your training to get more help from you.

You want to share your expertise to the reader in your

book. Show them why you are the one qualified to write the book as well as teach the course. Plan to highlight certain areas of your background, and your accumulated knowledge on the subject. Mention training and certifications you have earned that show you as a leader in your field or industry.

Tip

Keep a notebook or iPad handy at all times.

Review your course and make notes of what are the topics of interest in each lesson. Make special note of what the clients enjoyed or felt was the most useful to them—check out their testimonials!

Look over the marketing and promotional materials used for your course. What is highlighted? This needs to be a focus in the content covered in the chapters, especially in the case study descriptions.

Check out your current resume or biography. What can be used in the book from your credentials that will distinguish you as the unique expert you are?

Book Contents

No matter what option you choose to use—nonfiction book or memoir—the contents will follow the established order of your training program. Of course, you may want to jump ahead or flash back in certain areas of the book, but the main focus is on what's taught by you and the results the reader will get.

Each lesson in the course becomes a chapter in the book. Refer to the syllabus of your training program and convert it into the book's contents, highlighting the most obvious thing that is achieved in each class. This will be the focus of attention in each chapter: Call attention to the important points of the lesson and what will be achieved when completed.

An ideal number of chapters would be ten to twelve. In order to convert the course into this amount of content, you might have to break up some lessons into two or more chapters. Ultimately, it's decided by the length of the program, e.g., if it's a three-part training, then take each part and break it into three to four chapters.

On average, each chapter should be about 2,000 to 2,500 words, which adds up to approximately ten to twelve pages for each chapter (based on an average of 200 to 300 words per page). This makes an industry-standard-sized nonfiction self-help or how-to book of 100 to 120 pages and makes the book an excellent read for someone getting acquainted with your program, motivating readers to take it.

Your book literally becomes the first step a future client would take before working with you. It's a "vetting" tool for both the reader (future client) and you, the instructor. They learn about you, your methods, and the basic principles of your training program. On the flip side, you can determine if the person would make a good fit as a client for your offered course.

Tip

Follow this outline to begin drafting each chapter based on the lessons in your course. Fill in as much information as you can on your first run through. Remember, each chapter needs to engage the reader and "sell" them on the lesson material covered at the same time, in order for them to want to take your course.

Also note, you do not have to go in any order when outlining and writing the chapters. Start with ones that are easier for you to work with, or perhaps represent your favorite lessons in your training program.

Book Chapter Outline

Chapter What and Why: One or two paragraphs covering the what and why of the lesson that will be covered in the chapter. This introduces the reader to the subject matter.

Lesson Description: Tell main points of the lesson and use content from actual training material. Be sure to only use parts of the lesson that would interest the reader the most in order to get them motivated to take the course.

Case Study: The best material to highlight in each chapter are case studies from clients who have successfully completed your program. Breakdown the client's needs or concerns, how they were addressed, and what solution was achieved. Always mention your unique approach to the client's situation and how they benefited from this lesson.

Share Insight: After the case study (or each one

mentioned), share feedback of what this meant to you as a course instructor. What are the takeaways? Review how your client felt from taking the lesson. What was the overall outcome from your perspective as well as theirs?

Recommendations: How can the reader benefit from the lesson (and the entire program). This can be approached in two ways: *1)* Self-Help, by giving inspiration and encouragement, or *2)* How-To, by giving tips and tools (may refer to Reference Guide in the back of the book).

Chapter Recap: Short review of the chapter in at least three sentences (one paragraph) and as much as two to three paragraphs.

Lead into Next Chapter: Encourage the reader to go onto the next chapter. Highlight what's coming and what the next lesson in the course will cover from the overall training program. Do this in at least three sentences (one paragraph) and as much as two to three paragraphs.

Book For Course Marketing

Building your credibility in your field is paramount. You can easily achieve it by joining industry organizations and groups, and by attending conferences and summits. Think of the big names in your training niche; ever wondered what makes them so big?

Aside from their expertise, background and insights, they all have one thing in common: their names appear everywhere. This is what a book helps a trainer to achieve, to share their expertise on a larger scale beyond the audience they've built through their established client base.

You want to make sure you're the one everyone's talking about when there are other trainers out there in your field. It's all about the power of association. Everyone else could be talking about their training business through social media, but what if an international magazine or popular podcast is talking about you and your book?

Getting your name and your book featured in publications, or speaking as a guest on the hottest podcasts is the kind of exposure that turns heads and makes you the go-to expert in your field. Be the trainer everyone wants to work with.

A book helps you to create "social proof" of your training abilities. It instantly boosts your credibility because people tend to trust experts who are authors and have their book in the spotlight—whether it's the general public or your specific field of expertise.

Your book makes you stand out from the multitude of other trainers. It brings more eyes on your training program, and more eyes means more leads, more clients, and a significant boost in your business.

Tip

Getting your book out to establish your social proof is best done when using vehicles that bring fast and consistent results. These two following methods are known to build author visibility like no other.

1) Being seen in the media is one of the most effective ways to build your credibility, and it's not that hard to achieve when following the correct course of action.

2) Another tactic is being heard (and seen) on podcasts. This practice has grown in recent years. You can see immediate results and it's easily achieved through podcast opportunities for authors on a multitude of platforms.

Both of these approaches add a bonus to your overall media-building strategy. Print, visual, or audible coverage can all be transformed into effective marketing materials for your training program.

Examples include highlights on your website and in blog posts and features on media pages and in press kits, as well as mentions in brochures, flyers and event handouts. Media coverage also makes for excellent content in social media posts to build author credibility and a professional reputation. Print articles can be effectively used as materials being handed out at book signings and industry events.

Like the previously mentioned media coverage, you can repurpose audios and videos of podcast episodes. Featuring them on website pages and in blog posts as well as in emailed newsletters are some of the most recommended ways to use them. Other marketing methods include highlighting them on your YouTube channel and your Amazon book sales page as A+ content video replays.

My Course Transfer

As I mentioned earlier in this chapter, using yourself as an example is the best way to convince the reader of your expertise and qualifications. One of the most effective ways is to become a contributing author to an anthology book in your area of expertise, like I've done here with this coauthored book.

My specialty happens to be with self-help and how-to books. I'm writing this chapter based on the one-on-one training I do with my clients at my *BASS – Book Author Support Service*™ who happen to be mostly nonfiction and memoir writers. When I work with an author, I guide them through my *Authorpreneur System*™, showing them the steps to write, publish and market a successful nonfiction book or teaching memoir. I've transferred what I do for my clients into the materials described in this chapter.

Tip

If I can do it, you can do it too. You already have all the material for your book at your fingertips. It's all in your course. You just have to transfer the content of your training program to create your manuscript. Using the two outlines provided in this chapter is all you need to start writing your book today.

If you want additional help turning your course into a book and have interest in the *Authorpreneur System*™ described above, please refer to my author biography at the end of this chapter for the link to my *BASS for Authors*™ website.

Linda Berry is the owner of BASS—Book Author Support Service™. *She is a multiple #1 best-selling author with many books to her credit, including how-to and self-help, inspirational, business, and her Authorpreneur System*™ *book series. Find out more about Linda's BASS*™ *business and reach her at www.BASSfor-Authors.com*

13

THE "ONE" BUSINESS MODEL
BY RAM SHARMA

People should know that there is tremendous power in focusing on one business model, taking consistent action, having the vision to create long-term assets, and using the power of compounding to create generational business and wealth.

The Domino Effect

A domino can knock over another domino about 1.5 times larger than itself, and if dominoes are lined up, more and more power is amplified as each domino in the chain topples over. The first domino is only five millimeters high and one millimeter thick—so small that you need a pair of tweezers to put it in place.

This principle from the book *The ONE Thing* by Gary

Keller is precisely what helped me focus on publishing one book at a time consistently and regularly. Having done it for six years, and now completely outsourcing short fiction books, I have created a domino effect wherein these books sell one another and create a regular income day in and day out. This is the power of simple, focused, and consistent action.

In the following paragraphs, I will tell you about my journey to discovering my self-publishing model and the keys to effective online course creation.

Discovery of the "ONE" Business Model

Until you find your "ONE" thing, you will be all over the place. That's precisely what happened to me. My journey began when I suffered from a severe Lyme infection and had to face my mortality. At the time of infection, I worked in a fairly stable nine-to-five software architect job, designing software systems for the New Jersey police.

This was rather untimely, as just before the news of the infection, the following wonderful things had happened:

1. My wife and I became permanent residents of the United States.
2. I cleared Level 2 of the CFA (Chartered Financial Analyst) exam.
3. Our doctor confirmed that my wife and I were going to become parents for the second time.

Then my doctor told me about the infection. I had visited a week prior for testing, as I'd been experiencing frequent joint pains. As I'd never heard the term before, I typed "Lyme disease" into Google. About thirty minutes of research was enough to bring me from cloud nine to cloud zero.

Once the news sunk in, I was convinced the end of the world was near. I'd heard of two other cases of Lyme infections: one was put on recurring IV medications, and the other was completely bedridden. Both were much younger than me.

In desperation, I decided I needed to make money fast, as I firmly believed my days were numbered. Boy, when you look for quick money-making opportunities you get them by a truck load—promises of overnight bank accounts getting loaded, bright-and-shiny software systems, push-button riches, and everything in between. My mind spun. After grinding through the system, studying hard, getting an education from two top-ten colleges back home in India— including a master's in computer applications, Project Management Professional (PMP) certification, and two levels of CFA examination—moving to the US, and over ten years of software consulting assignments in some of the biggest financial and pharmaceutical industries, I still couldn't determine a way forward.

Thankfully, I did not die over the next few months, but I was certainly getting weaker than ever before. The spirituality that I had practiced so sincerely when I was in school came back to remind me that death is certain, but what matters is how one lives. So, I decided to start fresh. Rather than believing Lyme was going to kill me, I started looking for alternative healing systems. As I tried these methods, I gave up on searching for money-making offers, and luckily, my wonderful employers allowed me to work from home. Life went on. I spent many sleepless nights worried about my family, but I also started some simple daily practices: prayers, yoga, juicing, journaling, gratitude, qigong, and meditation. These gave me strength to do the routine things.

But the fact that I could make money online had been subconsciously implanted in my brain. I spent a few thousand dollars on "shiny objects" without a proper direction before I started working with a mentor and coach. I launched a product that sold 250-plus copies but wasn't sure where to go from there, as my coach retired.

Finding my "ONE" thing helped me move forward. Here is the goal-setting process I followed:

Someday Goal: Start by thinking about the most important Someday Goal in your life. What is the ONE thing that would be epic to do someday?

Five-Year Goal: Based on your Someday Goal, what's the ONE thing you can do in the next five years?

One-Year Goal: Based on your Five-Year Goal, what's the ONE thing you can do this year?

One-Month Goal: Based on your One-Year Goal, what's the ONE thing you can do this month?

One-Week Goal: Based on your One-Month Goal, what's the ONE thing you can do this week?

Daily Goal: Based on your One-Week Goal, what's the ONE thing you can do today?

Right Now: Based on your Daily Goal, what's the ONE thing you can do right now?

To start, I focused on "ONE" thing, publishing short fiction stories in small subgenres on Amazon's wonderful KDP platform. Over the last six years, that system gave me the freedom to spend time with my family and the compounding effect of financial security. After a series of optimizations, I have come to a point where I work only about one to two hours a week on this simple system. Now my goal is to create simple business systems that give me, my children, and my readers freedom to do things that matter most in life, along with a good amount of financial stability.

Accelerating Digital Entrepreneurship Through Course Creation

I firmly believe that the best and most effective way to create and grow my brand, serve more people, scale my business, and make more generational wealth is to package my publishing system into an easy-to-consume and transformative online course. According to a study conducted by Polaris Market Research, the global e-learning market reached a value of USD 214.26 billion in 2021, and experts project it will grow at a CAGR (compound annual growth rate) of 20.5 percent, potentially reaching USD 1,124.79 billion by 2030. The online learning boom is only going to grow over time as improved technology and AI-assisted tools are released, making it easier than ever to create courses.

When you create your course, you're solving problems for your customers based on your expertise, wisdom, and results you have achieved. You can become their time-saving friend as you show, step by step, the results you have achieved. While there are many AI-assisted "secret" ChatGPT prompts that are coming up with promises of the ability to create an entire course even if you know nothing about the niche, in my honest opinion, these are a complete waste of time—both your time and your audience's.

If you solve a genuine problem, one you have faced and overcame, that becomes the best product possible. The authenticity of such a product is incredibly valuable. Ideally, if the topic involves health, wealth, relationships, or spirituality, and overcoming pain (of health/relationship issues) or creating abundance (wealth through your successful business or connection to a higher power), these areas are universally applicable. Sharing your story will make your course powerful, unique, and precious.

There is nothing wrong with creating courses by researching the best techniques, but the longevity of a flagship product like Tony Robbins's Unleash the Power Within or Brian Tracy's Maximum Productivity comes from the life stories and struggles embedded within. They have used these systems to elevate their lives and then add on new techniques, as they are learning all the time.

As a course creator, you have a unique opportunity to

guide your audience, teach them and guide them toward their life's vision. And the best part? They'll pay you to be the person who expedites the process as long as you deliver high-quality work and results. To them, your expertise and results are valuable and will create a belief in your method.

The wisdom you get from those who've already "walked before you" can be way more powerful than systematic school/college learning. Although formal education is valuable, there is nothing like the hands-on experience of putting yourself out there, achieving results, and delivering life-transforming courses.

Lastly, the great thing about technological advances like Pubfunnels and AWeber, among other outstanding tools, is that you can have your course up and running quickly. The key is to package your knowledge, wisdom, story, and results in a framework that makes it easy to follow and successfully replicate.

Currently, I am creating a course that is based on the results of my self-publishing system. I am working on developing a method that enables individuals to start a great side hustle, step by step, even while prioritizing their primary job, family, and other interests. Follow the simple method to creating this wonderfully simple and scalable passive income side hustle system on my website.

In summary, focus on creating long-term assets and give great value to your readers/customers. It is better to do the things you love and spend time on what matters most: your loved ones. As I discovered, focusing on "ONE" thing—in this case, course creation—and taking consistent action will allow you to do so, as well as give back to the world and make others' lives more abundant.

———————

Ram built his one-person publishing house to over $400K in revenue and details his process at https://ramsharma.me.

14

SELL THEM WHAT THEY WANT; GIVE THEM WHAT THEY NEED

BY TED DEMOPOULOS

P eople buy what they want, but they rarely know what they need. This is especially true with knowledge products like courses.

If you are writing a course, you are the expert. You know what the students will need to succeed, and it's your job to put what they need in the course. However, if you don't also give them what they want, they won't engage with the course —whether that means buying it in the first place, signing up for a free course, registering at their school, etc.

Many course creators "shudder" at the word "expert." Expert doesn't mean the "best in the world" or the top "1 percent" or similar. It just means you have valuable information, and as a lower level expert, you may be the perfect person to write a course for beginners. In fact, world-class experts often can't relate to beginners, and therefore can't as effectively write a course for them. This is because of what is often called "the curse of knowledge": the more you know, the harder it is to relate to beginners. Most people are beginners, and most courses are aimed at beginners. And if you include beginners to intermediates, you have the vast majority of the market. In contrast, if you write a course for the top 1 or 2 percent in any area, your market will obviously be much smaller.

In my first job after graduate school, I was tasked with writing a course for the company's Linux-like system. The boss wanted the course to follow the outline of an existing and very successful course on the company's proprietary system. That is also what the customers wanted. What was wanted was obvious, as it often is.

I decided the course also needed two additional things: information on how to set up and use the internet protocol, and how to make the system robust and reliable, which basically means secure. This was before the internet had taken off and before we had to worry about hackers breaking into our systems. I felt strongly that this course needed this information for long-term success. I was the "expert" and was determined to give people what they needed, whether they knew it or not.

This was a hard sell to my boss, although I succeeded. I had to convince him of three things: first, that I could include what he and the customers wanted plus what I thought they needed and finish writing the course on time; second, that what I thought they needed was important; and third, that I could convince the students that it was indeed important.

The course was very successful and a long-term bestseller.

Around the same time, a brilliant man named Harry joined the company. One of his early tasks was to write a course on a complex system that he knew well but few others did. Harry was a true world-class expert on this system, and he knew exactly what students needed.

He proceeded to develop the course ignoring what students and the boss wanted in the class. After all, he was the expert and legitimately knew more than the future students and "the boss." Let's just shorten the story and say that not only was the course not remotely successful— almost no one signed up to take it—but Harry also ended up as a very short-term employee at this company! The term "disaster" comes to mind. He refused to include what people wanted.

Today my courses are more on the business and entrepreneurial side, but the same principles apply.

For example, in my best-selling course on how to be a consultant, everyone wants to know two things: how to get clients, and what to charge them. And yes, these are important topics that I cover, but there are other equally, if not more, important topics that few people think about initially that are needed for long-term success. These include thinking about what type of consultancy one wants to create, how the consultancy will evolve over time—and they all do —and a myriad of other topics.

I sell them what they want, how to get clients and set pricing, and also give them what they need for success in consulting. The course sells well, as I include what they want, and the students are successful because I also cover what they need.

A course I am working on now is on startup companies. There are two topics of extreme interest to most of my audience for this course. The first is on funding, with an emphasis on venture capital. The second is on how to come up with a great idea for the startup company. That is what people want.

Funding is important, of course, and I'm covering that, including venture capital. What people really need is to understand that most startups by far should not pursue venture capital, and not only don't need it but shouldn't chase it. In fact, "venture capital" is a rather new concept—it didn't even exist in its current form until the 1990s. What people need to know is about other funding options, including bootstrapping, angel investing, equity crowdfunding, and more. Bootstrapping, starting with existing resources, is the most important topic for most, and I cover it extensively, but few people actually want that, at least initially.

As mentioned, the importance of having a great company idea is something people want to know a lot about, and although important, is of secondary importance at best. Ideas very often need to change! For example, Starbucks didn't originally sell brewed coffee; they sold espresso makers and coffee beans. Nokia started as a papermill and later sold rubber goods and other products before entering the telecommunications and cell phone space. HP wasn't originally a computer company. Wrigley didn't start out selling gum, and Suzuki started as an inventor and seller of weaving loom machines.

A lot of companies start with an idea, but what leads them to their ultimate success involves pivoting. Pivoting is simply changing direction when the current idea and strategy around it is not delivering the desired results. It is rare for a startup's initial idea to survive intact, and pivoting, whether minor or major, is usually required for success.

People want to know about funding, especially venture capital, and about having a great idea for a startup. I "sell" them on that. What they really need is a myriad of other topics, including other funding models, the importance of being willing to pivot, teamwork, and long-term vision. I give them that in the course.

What if you don't think you are "selling"? Maybe your course is implemented as a series of emails people can sign up to receive for free. Or maybe it is a series of YouTube videos with no registration required. The exact same concepts apply! You need to sell them on the idea of taking your course. And as a friend of mine says, you need to sell the free stuff as much as the paid stuff.

If we are going to sell people what they want, how do we know what they want? You may simply know because you have been in your field for a long time. If not, and even if you think you know, just ask people! It's really that simple. You might engage with your colleagues, talk to people at conferences and other events, do online research, or even run a simple online poll.

Now, how do you know what they need? As an expert in the field, you may simply know or feel you know. Even if you do, I suggest looking at what people who are successfully doing what the course teaches are doing. In other words, research what successful people are doing.

"Sell them what they want; give them what they need" is the model for course success. Skip either of these, and you may have a course that doesn't sell well, or results in people only having limited success.

Ted Demopoulos is an entrepreneur, best-selling author, and a long-time consultant. You can learn more about Ted at TedDemop.com.

15

YOUR LONELY ROOM
BY ROBERT WOOD ANDERSON

W hen I arrived at my military/religious high school for the first time, I was quietly afraid of what awaited me. I was tall, skinny, and away from home. The irony is that I asked to go away to school, for I was a scaredy cat and afraid of my shadow.

On day one, it became clear that the seniors were in charge and the sophomores were the hammers taking out their first-year harassment on the newbies. And, on command, I became a member of the fourth-form sophomoric retribution squad. I had earned it, don't you know?

To say that I was full of myself is too obvious, but it was a cover. It's the bully's disguise to hide fear and self-doubt. On the outside, I was fearless. On the inside, I was a coward fortified by the collective forth-form hive. Thank God I grew out of it. But it wasn't easy.

There was an elite group drill team at the school. It was

considered the best drill squad in the nation, and that moniker had been attached to it for years. Acceptance on the Squad included physically and mentally taxing tryouts. There were other factors, to be sure, yet the acceptance process was meant to cull the weak of spirit by testing determination with hardship, ridicule, and sleepless nights. Anyone who has been through boot camp will understand that a soldier's spirit must be torn down to test his mettle and draw him closer to his suffering comrades. Thus is a team made.

The point of this story becomes clear when you know that I was doubtful I would make the grade. I've mentioned that I'm tall but was no basketball player. My monikers at school were "Tree" and "Spaz." Both names were appropriate at the time. Who was I to seek the honor of trying out and maybe even being accepted on the Squad? Could I handle the long, daily, secret training? Was I worth the honor? Was it worth it to go through it all only to be cut? If cut, could I manage the shame? These questions nagged me so much that I almost gave up trying. But after toughing out the months-long training and surviving "Hell Night," I was tapped on the back, signifying my acceptance into the Squad.

Was it worth it? Certainly, if only for finding the fortitude to see it through. They still called me "Tree," but "Spaz" died a righteous death.

My story is not unusual. Self-doubt is my constant companion. The difference now is I can easily shut down that nagging voice and recognize that nothing worthwhile comes from assuming I'm unworthy or ill-equipped for a task. I'll get the training I need if I do fall short.

Introspection is mandatory, but giving up before assessing one's strengths and weaknesses is unacceptable.

Ultimately, I may discover that whatever the challenge, it's not for me. I may not want to do the hard work to succeed. I may not have the required talent. I may be grasping the most recent shiny object flashing before my eyes.

But I need to investigate those possibilities. Instead of assuming inadequacy, it's time to consider my skills with open eyes and try not to diminish the talents given to me.

Let's see how this approach might help you develop your self-esteem. This internal "war to the knife" can rapidly turn your self-doubt into positive action.

The expression "war to the knife" refers to adjusting one's battle plan during a conflagration. Starting high above with wide-area bombardment, then shifting to cannon fire, and then to tank battalions, the battle often is decided in hand-to-hand combat. The triumphant army is the one that handles the blade mano a mano. The battle gets down to a struggle with yourself.

Jackie Gleason used to say, "It's bigger than the both of us." Your course's premise may seem great, but it's possibly full of mush and extraneous information.

When you started putting your course on paper, your creative mind had no collar or leash. You may have had a great start, but almost always, it's a bad place to end. You may think you created a masterpiece on the first pass, and if you do, hoorah! More likely, your idea needs refinement. Don't think your initial attempt is perfect and race to promote. And don't get in the dumps, clutching pearls and giving up hope. Both are wrong.

First, if you aren't a genius, like I am not, there must be a way to improve your content so it is pithy. Chances are a lot of excess words can be cut, making your presentation crisp and eye-opening instead of sleep-inducing.

Now, if you are fighting a battle of self-doubt, wondering if you are worthy of offering your course to the world, you aren't alone. Much has been written on how to overcome inferiority. I have my cures as well. Hopefully, I can help you stick a finger in the world's eye and strut your stuff to your best audience.

Make no mistake. Your course must identify a real problem and demonstrate a path to an achievable solution. The question is, why are you holding back? So here it goes:

Look in the mirror. No, don't pretend. Really gaze into your eyes and be silent for a while. Let yourself remember how you felt before you finally decided to create a course. Surely, you have subscribed to others' courses that have helped you. Remember the relief and joy when the thing holding you back was defeated because of the course you bought? Think of one imaginary student who would be over-joyed and relieved to find a practical way to solve a problem you have conquered. You have a conversation with that one person and be successful, right?

If you struggle with inadequacy and doubt your exper-tise, consider the hundreds of thousands who feel the same way and do nothing to take the first step. You've never heard from them and never will. They never took the first step. You must take that first step. Without it, there will be nothing. Set aside the journey's difficulties for a while and get started. If you flop, give it a good cry and put a Band-Aid on your skinned knees. Get up and start again. It takes work and dedication. Confidence may be fleeting or never come, but you can be certain that doing nothing will become a heavier weight around your neck each day.

> *"Don't sit there in your lonely room looking back inside at gloom. Mama, that's not where you belong."*
>
> — *"TAKE A GIANT STEP"* BY TAJ MAHAL

Hopefully your course is meant to solve a problem many people face. How wonderful to touch all their hearts. That is an extraordinary gift. And it's yours to give. One person helped may become thousands helped just because you dared to look into your eyes and see the purpose of your course.

That purpose is to save others from stumbling, to give them the code that helped you move ahead. It's a code that worked for you, a solution for many people's problems.

Hand in hand with the problem is the solution. It is one thing to connect with an eager audience and another to leave them satisfied. Satisfaction means knowing the steps that can eliminate the problem. The solution is your expertise and the effort your students bring to the game. Your solution may be common sense to you but unknown to your audience.

So, it's time to put the mirror away. Confidence has been restored. Get those bullet points in order and flesh out your script. You have walked the path. You are the expert. Embrace your knowledge with modesty, and your audience will stay with you.

Now, say out loud, "I can help someone!" Say it and mean it, and put the knife down. Your battle with yourself is finished. Get started rewriting and editing. Your audience is waiting for you, not someone else!

———

Best-selling author Robert Wood Anderson's thrillers include Popoford's Run 3-Book Thriller-Paranormal Series. His most recent book, Crush His Heart, a Max Augustine Thriller, has received highly favorable reviews. Robert has achieved best-selling Amazon status and is a Global Book Award Winner. His latest book, 2433, is a religious, dystopian epic, and available soon. You can connect with Robert at rwa-author.ink

16

OVERCOMING IMPOSTER SYNDROME: FOUR SECRETS FOR AUTHENTIC COURSE CREATION

BY PAUL T NEUSTROM

Allow me to open this chapter by sharing an inspiring tale, one I often tell clients who desire to craft an original course endeavoring to overcome the biggest dream killer, imposter syndrome.

In the bustling heart of Manhattan, a young man named Leo dreamed of making his presence known in the fashion industry. His sketches were bold, his designs innovative, and his passion for fashion burned brightly. But breaking into the competitive world of New York's fashion scene proved to be an insurmountable challenge. Lacking connections, key suppliers, and a wealthy clientele, Leo found himself on the outside, looking in.

One chilly autumn evening, while wandering through the vibrant streets of the Garment District, Leo slipped inside a small, nondescript café, seeking refuge from a chilly night. As he drank his warm coffee, he noticed an elderly man sitting in the back corner, engrossed in an older fashion magazine.

Intrigued by the man's presence and noticeable similar interest, Leo struck up a conversation. The distinguished gentleman introduced himself as Henry, a retired writer for the renowned *Esquire* magazine. As they talked, Leo shared his aspirations and struggles.

Henry listened intently, his eyes twinkling with a mix of nostalgia and understanding. He began by explaining, "Entering the fashion industry can be challenging, so here is something that possibly will assist your journey."

Henry related a memory from his years at the magazine: Thomas was once an up-and-coming, talented designer facing similar obstacles as Leo in this competitive environment. Yet he struggled to gain any ground because of a lack of connections, resources, and understanding what the market truly desired. Despite all his hard work, he could not break through.

"One day," Henry continued, "Thomas decided to change his approach. Instead of trying to sell his designs into the industry, he became a tailor at one of New York's most respected clothiers and worked directly with clients— learning their likes, dislikes, and needs. He discovered the issues and preferences people had with their clothing."

Through his work, Thomas began to notice a niche that was underserved. He observed that many clients sought custom, high-quality clothing that combined traditional craftsmanship with modern aesthetics. By listening to their feedback and understanding their needs, Thomas identified a unique opportunity, and he served it well.

"Instead of guessing what the market wanted," Henry explained, "Thomas let the market tell him. He learned to put aside his ego and focused on serving his clients' needs. When he finally launched his own brand, it wasn't just another line of clothing—it was a solution to a problem, a response to a demand. His brand quickly gained recognition and success because it resonated deeply with what people were looking for."

Leo was inspired by Thomas's tale. Realizing his approach needed a complete overhaul, he secured an apprenticeship with one of the Garment District's prestigious men's stores. The young designer in training devoted himself to mastering the craft, and he gained valuable insights into fashion preferences and pain points, building strong relationships and refining his abilities.

Through careful observation, he identified a niche in the market for sustainable, high-end suits. His discerning attention to detail and unwavering commitment to the craft resonated with customers. This led to the establishment of Leo's own brand, built on a foundation of trust and appreciation for his selfless dedication to fulfilling his clients' discerning needs.

This example provided a perfect analogy for a client of mine, who struggled for months to create a course. Inspired by hearing Henry's "pearls of wisdom," the client realized he needed to pivot away from guesswork. By engaging more directly with students, he started creating content tailored specifically to their struggles and aspirations. This shift made all the difference, allowing him to fulfill the real needs of his students.

The moral of the story: Success lies in understanding and meeting people's needs rather than imposing our own perceptions on them. Applying this lesson to course development ensures that your content will resonate deeply and provide genuine value.

This story is inspired from my own experience when I was twenty-five years old. I worked for Whittle Communications, the parent company of *Esquire* magazine. We were the largest publisher of specialty print magazines at that time. I learned through an entry-level mentorship, which allowed me to succeed as the assistant to the vice president of marketing.

Whenever we did national sell-ins with our sales force of twenty-eight across the country, we would always listen to our customers' wants, needs, and desires first, before trying to serve them with our own "great ideas."

Since learning this, I have consistently dedicated myself to the pursuit of publishing.

It is not enough to simply impart knowledge. You must also emotionally connect with your audience, satisfy their needs, and make a powerful impression.

Discovering Your Audience's Voice

Finding what I refer to as "the voice of my audience" was an extremely transformative experience for me as an award-winning author and keynote speaker. Once I discovered this, my brain completely rewired itself so all my content fit seamlessly within one framework that made an important difference in people's lives.

These four secrets will help you create a powerful presentation and dynamic interaction. Following these communication principles will ensure that your course resonates deeply with your learners and provides them with practical value.

1. Start with a story that connects: Use relatable experiences or personal stories to create connection and engagement. A compelling narrative, whether it is your own or someone else's, sets the stage for relational learning.

2. Tell them the adventure: Take your audience on a quest through the course, highlighting challenges, learning opportunities, and possible transformations. You can use the journey outline as a way to inform and inspire your audience, while highlighting the benefits of their interactive expedition.

3. Deliver on the promise: Consistency is of the utmost importance; clearly establish objectives, develop engaging content that meets these parameters, include real-life examples where possible, and listen to student feedback. These are the keys to delivering on what was promised at the outset of each lesson.

4. End each session by giving them practical strategies or steps to implement immediately. Use checklists, templates, and challenges to help students learn beyond the classroom.

Powerful Course Creation Strategies

Your voice is at the core of both writing and speaking, and honing it will benefit both areas. The ability to share stories to audiences and readers has become my trademark. The words we choose, whether written or spoken, carry our thoughts and feelings into the hearts of others, leaving a lasting impact.

By incorporating vision, originality, inspiration, creativity, and embodiment, instructors create courses that resonate and transform lives.

My Quest for Authenticity

After leaving a men's monastery where I had lived for two years, I embarked on an unexpected and challenging journey. Feeling lost without any sense of purpose or meaning in my life, reading classics such as Viktor Frankl's *Man's Search for Meaning* taught me a valuable lesson.

> *One can overcome any obstacle by finding their purpose and direction in life.*

My goal was to finish my book that would record all the

lessons from my life's journey. Although I was only halfway done with my manuscript, I overcame my fears and doubts to finish writing my memoir and discover my purpose: helping others to find a prosperous and rewarding life.

Common Struggles in Course Development

As a course creator, here are some of the biggest challenges to overcome; understanding these common pitfalls will give you a unique advantage.

Lack of Feedback

Course creators who lack feedback from potential students often struggle with content uncertainty. One way of combating this uncertainty is forming a beta group of core students to voice their needs and help identify challenges through an interactive learning process. Leveraging such groups not only allows course creators to refine course content more effectively but also fosters community and engagement within their learning experience. Leo, the young fashion designer, had to lower himself and start at a more humble beginning, and the rewards were what led to his exaltation.

Building Community is Key

It is next to impossible to create a course in a vacuum.

Building a course requires more than simply imparting knowledge; it involves cultivating an audience of followers. Gaining an understanding of their struggles and needs allows you to custom-design the content to provide maximum value; this approach doesn't rely on guesswork but creates interaction through genuine engagement with attendees.

Imposter Syndrome

Experience is often a barrier for those starting to create courses for the first time, while even experienced course creators can reach a plateau and become stuck. This is a significant barrier for entrepreneurs, instilling a deep-seated fear of failure and self-doubt. Despite their accomplishments and skills, many feel like frauds and fear being exposed as inadequate. This psychological pattern hinders originality and innovation. This is broken by discovering your own voice, which will foster creativity.

Poor Engagement

The students may find it difficult to focus and retain large amounts of information. You have a dual role as an educator and a facilitator. Your task is to include challenges and gamification into your course. Encourage participants to face adversity to find their full potential. To create a course that is unique and memorable, you need to be able to relate to, identify with, and satisfy your people.

Finding your voice in course creation can have a profound impact. By visualizing goals, organizing thoughts, injecting personality, creating value, and engaging with your audience, you can become a skilled course creator. Embrace your unique gifts, overcome your fears, and step into the extraordinary future that awaits you.

To effectively engage your class, consider the **D.A.R.E.S.** delivery:

D - **Discover and Develop the Concept:** Briefly explain the point or idea.

A - **Acknowledge Key Insights:** Summarize the key insights from the discussion.

R - **Respond:** Validate their responses through open-ended questions.

E - **Encourage Discussion:** Facilitate group dialogue and sharing.

S - **Set an Activity:** Introduce a short activity to apply the concepts.

The V.O.I.C.E. Framework for Authentic Course Creation consists of: Vision, Originality, Inspiration, Creativity, Embodiment. This is the blueprint for developing powerfully engaging courses.

Vision: Aligning your course with correct perception ensures its purpose, values, and desired impact are clear and impactful.

Originality: Embrace your individuality and genuine self-expression. Your individual viewpoint is what makes your course unique and engaging.

Inspiration: Foster dynamic learning through activities

that inspire you. Seek diverse sources, nurture curiosity, and keep a journal of ideas to fuel and document your course content creation.

Creativity: Experimenting with different ideas and communication methods enhances the effectiveness of your teaching and keeps your audience involved and engaged.

Embodiment: Fully embrace and practice the principles you teach. Authenticity in teaching comes from living the lessons you share with your audience. It also allows them to begin to apply these interactions.

Remember, the voice of your customer is your most powerful teacher. Discover it, serve it, and watch your impact and influence grow.

My book, *Death of a Yellow Page Salesman*, was selected as the curriculum for a college entrepreneurship class because of its innovative marketing principles, emphasizing the significance of relationships in the digital age. It inspires individuals to find fulfillment in business through meaningful human interactions, leaving a legacy of purpose and overflow in life.

Paul is an International #1 Best-Selling and Award-Winning Author, Keynote Speaker, and founder of the Publish, Speak, and Prosper movement. He helps people discover their voice and write compelling content that resonates, inspires, and creates authority. You can visit his website atPaulNeustrom.com to get autographed copies of his books and discover valuable resources.

17

KEYS TO CULTIVATING TRANSFORMATION

BY ARABA AFENYI-ANNAN

"What?" I exclaimed with wide eyes. "How am I supposed to know how to do this after one module?"

With clenched fists and a racing heart, I reread the assignment on my computer screen. Then, feeling defeated, I slumped down and groaned. I had reached the end of the first module in a twelve-week online course on storytelling for business. With this less-than-ideal start, I wondered if this program was right for me. Little did I know that at the end of the twelve weeks, I would eagerly continue on to the next program offering, grateful for the learning and insight I gained from the class.

This short course taught me much more than how to use stories in my business. It pointed out in neon lights the perfectionism I thought I had cured was there lingering in the shadows. The outburst I described came from nearly paralyzing anxiety that prevented me from completing the class assignments at the end of each module for weeks. These assignments asked me to post videos of myself telling stories. I cringe thinking about the hours I spent recording and rerecording, trying to "perfect" my beginner video attempts until they were suitable to share with others. The class shed light on the beliefs and fears that held me back from fully putting myself and my message out into the world.

In a relatively short period of time, I became someone who could embrace this system of learning and utilize the components that worked best for me. As a retired physician, learning and teaching were familiar to me. Now, as a spiritual counselor and parenting coach who has designed transformational programs, I better understand the overarching principles and components that made this three-month online course successful. The primary principle that anyone who is interested in creating an online transformational course should remember is: Real-life application of information creates transformation.

In my mind, the distinguishing features of a transformational course are: 1) it provides skills and tools that can be used in a specific aspect of life, like business; 2) it offers highly experiential learning of practical information that can be applied to any area of life; and 3) it creates a tangible shift in the user's mind, beliefs, thoughts, or approach that improves their quality and/or experience of life. In my view, a course's success in achieving these criteria is determined by three components: Simplify, Structure, and Supplement.

Simplify

All of us have constraints in our life, whether it is time, energy, or resources (like money). Sometimes the constraints are in all three areas. When we take time to simplify course material, it honors our clients' time as valuable, recognizes their energy and efforts, and not least of all, acknowledges the financial investment they have made in the course and themselves. The edict to simplify often feels difficult when we are passionate about our offering and message. We have become experts in our topic through the school of life and likely other training. Being immersed in our field, we typically forget that what now feels obvious to us is, well, brand new to a beginner. Somewhere in our conscious mind, we recognize this and attempt to teach material at a Level 5 instead of Level 10. However, we really need to begin our teaching at a Level 2 or 3. The vast majority of people want to be passive learners, without making additional efforts to learn once they have signed up for a course.

To have a successful course, it is important to address potential barriers to learning, such as language and terminology, and improve a course's effectiveness. Removing these types of barriers successfully begins with identifying the critical problem(s) your course solves. Then, identify the immediate needs of your target audience. Next, drill both of these down to their essence, using very basic sentences. Finally, double-check that the problem(s) your course solves aligns with the problems your target audience wants solved now rather than later. If clear alignment is missing, continue to revise your curriculum until there is significant overlap. People need their immediate issues addressed before they can go deeper or take in new information.

Remember to use simple language, not highfalutin words that a fifth grader would have difficulty comprehending. Some marketing experts suggest using the sixth to eighth grade reading and comprehension level as a benchmark. The purpose of this type of benchmark is to ensure that your message and course content are easily understood by your widest possible target audience. Use whatever level of reading and comprehension that is best suited for this purpose. Without knowing your audience's familiarity with your course's subject area, their level of understanding of the material, their goals for learning the information, or their preferred learning styles, simplicity will always win the day.

Finally, an aspect of simplicity I had not previously considered but found extremely effective in my storytelling course was providing the information in short, concise lessons, no more than ten minutes long. There was no sense of overwhelm or resistance to doing the work. In fact, it felt fun. No matter how busy I was, I could fit a five-to-seven-minute lesson into my day. I could easily complete two or three lessons while sitting in the car pickup line at my children's school. It was rarely a problem to complete a module each week, and over the course of the twelve weeks, these repeated short interactions with the material led to high retention of the course content. I always had a sense of moving forward, a step at a time, never stuck or stagnant. This felt empowering and made me confident that no matter where I started from, I could master the material.

Structure

Structure is a critical component to the success of all endeavors. In a transformational course, the outline creates the container where transformation is possible and the step-by-step roadmap that leads your audience from point A, where they currently are, to point B, where they would like to be. The container is the place where your vision of possibilities meets your participants' hopes, dreams, and fears. Even the most skeptical, who believe that transformation is possible but not for them, find reassurance in knowing that a pathway to their hearts' desires exists.

In my storytelling class, I noticed the lessons were structured in a particular way. I learned about this pattern years ago from Sandy Grear, Vice President of Communications, Member Engagement, and Professional Development for a physician organization. Throughout our public speaking and spokesperson training, we were advised to "1) Tell them what you're going to tell them; 2) Tell them; and 3) Tell them what you told them." This quote, often attributed to Aristotle, is alternately known as the Three Tell mechanism and the "tell 'em" approach. It is a tool used in speech writing and delivery, as well as giving presentations. While the method may sound straightforward, perhaps even obvious, it is a masterful technique. When used, it creates clarity and adds structure to your message. By repeatedly summarizing your key points, your audience walks away remembering your message.

Another key structural component of a transformational course is based on the Kolb experiential learning theory. The theory describes a four-stage learning cycle that is characterized by: 1) "Doing"—learning by personal experience; 2) "Reflecting"—observing and finding meaning in the experience; 3) "Thinking"—connecting the experience to existing concepts, then generating new ideas; and 4) "Redoing"—using insight from the previous stages, experimenting with new ideas, and evaluating if a desired outcome was achieved. By creating a course that addresses each stage in this cycle, you utilize aspects of adaptive learning to tailor and deliver a personalized user learning experience. This structure, combined with the "tell 'em" approach, optimizes your course as the container and roadmap for transformation.

Supplement

Many people believe that course content is the primary determinant to the success of their course and that the second is course presentation. Successful transformational courses may or may not follow this model. Rather, they understand the value of supplementing their course content with resources that enhance a participant's experience, foster connections among participants, and create a sense of community, recognizing that transformation does not happen where interconnectedness and trust are absent. Often, these are simple things, like providing a list of resources and additional materials for those who would like to deepen their course experience or remembering to enable closed captioning at the start of any recording so a transcript can be generated and then made accessible to everyone. Consider written summaries highlighting key takeaways from course modules.

Sharing personal stories and experience helps participants feel safe sharing their own challenges and vulnerabilities and promotes connection within the group. People often feel isolated and unseen. The act of "seeing" another person and being truly "seen" can be deeply healing in and of itself. Courses that include a weekly touchpoint for Q&A and group coaching encourage community and connection. Provide ground rules or credos that govern the respectful, life-affirming types of communication acceptable in the community. Often, the care and effort taken on these seemingly small details can have life-changing impacts.

In summary, developing a successful, transformational online course depends on a number of things, including simplicity, structure, and skillful supplementation to enhance the participant experience. Key features of a successful course include being practical and widely applicable, as well as offering real-life, hands-on, experiential learning. Participants must feel capable of successfully comprehending, mastering, and applying the course content to improve the quality of their lives and their experience. This type of course must include reflective, conceptional, and evaluative processes, engender trust, and build a sense of community. Shorter is sweeter, and practice makes perfect. Or, as in this case, practice makes transformation.

Araba Afenyi-Annan, MD, MPH, is a teacher, speaker, spiritual counselor, and parenting coach who can be reached at her website:www.hooray4healing.com.

18

CLARITY IN COURSE CREATION: FROM CONFUSION TO EMPOWERMENT

BY SHIHAN SHERIFF

Have you ever found yourself drowning in a sea of complex concepts, feeling like you'll never be able to grasp the subject at hand? As someone who has navigated the treacherous waters of confusion and emerged victorious on the shores of clarity, I can assure you that you're not alone.

When I first ventured into the world of commerce and accounting, I was overwhelmed by the sheer volume of unfamiliar terms and intricate ideas. I remember the long nights spent hunched over textbooks, my mind spinning with numbers and formulas that seemed to blur together on the page. The frustration and self-doubt were palpable, and I feared I might never truly understand these subjects.

"Amid my struggle, a guiding light appeared in the form of a strong belief that I could do this and the unwavering support of my loved ones."

Through the encouragement of family and friends and the power of breaking down complex concepts into manageable pieces, I slowly but surely built a foundation of knowledge that improved my academic performance and ignited a deep passion for teaching others.

This journey, filled with challenges and triumphs, taught me an invaluable lesson: clarity is the key to unlocking understanding and empowering learners from all walks of life. By prioritizing accessibility and simplicity in our course creation, we can open doors that may have previously seemed closed and help students from diverse backgrounds achieve their full potential.

As I transitioned from student to educator, I witnessed firsthand the transformative impact of explicit, engaging instruction. I vividly recall working with a client who was grappling with the intricacies of financial ratios. The confusion and frustration in their eyes mirrored my own experiences as a student. However, by guiding them through a real-world case study and demonstrating the practical application of these concepts, I watched as the fog of confusion lifted. It was replaced by a sense of confidence and understanding that was truly remarkable.

This experience, and countless others like it, has reinforced my belief in the power of clarity to bridge the gap between theory and practice, making even the most complex subjects accessible to learners from all corners of the globe.

So, how can you harness the power of clarity in your own course creation? It begins with a deep understanding of your audience and their unique needs. Take the time to identify the core concepts you wish to convey and break them down into manageable segments that can be easily understood and applied.

> *"Use relatable examples, thought-provoking case studies, and engaging visuals to bring your content to life, considering your students' diverse backgrounds and learning styles."*

By creating accessible, inclusive, and culturally relevant content, you can ensure that your course resonates with learners from around the world. Engage your students through interactive elements such as quizzes, reflection prompts, and hands-on exercises, and leverage advanced technological tools to measure learner engagement and success.

As you develop your course, seek feedback from colleagues, mentors, and beta testers, and be open to adapting your content based on their insights and suggestions. Embrace a continuous improvement mindset, and never stop learning and growing as an educator.

Key Takeaways:

- Clarity is essential for unlocking understanding and empowering learners from all backgrounds.
- Break down complex concepts into manageable segments and use relatable examples to make learning accessible.
- Engage learners through interactive elements and foster a sense of community and collaboration.
- Continuously seek feedback and adapt your course based on learner needs and industry trends.
- Embrace a mindset of lifelong learning and growth as an educator.

Conclusion:

Creating a course that empowers learners to navigate the journey from confusion to clarity is both a privilege and a responsibility. By prioritizing clarity, accessibility, and inclusivity in our course creation, we impart knowledge and foster a love for learning that can transform lives.

As you embark on your own course creation journey, remember that your unique perspective and experiences are your greatest assets. Embrace the power of storytelling, and let your passion for teaching shine through in every aspect of your course.

The path to clarity may be challenging, but it is also incredibly rewarding. With each barrier you break down, each mind you inspire, and each life you touch, you are making a difference that extends far beyond the confines of your course.

So embrace the journey, trust the process, and never stop learning. Your dedication to clarity, empowerment, and life-long growth will inspire generations of learners and help shape a future where education is accessible, engaging, and transformative for all.

Action Items:

1. Reflect on your own learning experiences and identify moments when clarity (or lack thereof) significantly impacted your understanding. Use these insights to inform your course creation process.

2. Conduct thorough audience research to understand your potential students' diverse needs, backgrounds, and learning styles. Use this information to create content that is accessible, inclusive, and culturally relevant.

3. Develop a range of interactive elements for your course, such as quizzes, discussion prompts, case studies, and practical assignments. Continuously evaluate and refine these elements based on student feedback and engagement levels.

4. Join or create an online community of course creators to share experiences, challenges, and successes. Engage in discussions, offer support, and learn from the insights of others in your field.

5. Commit to ongoing professional development by

attending workshops, conferences, and webinars. Explore advanced technological tools and resources that can enhance your course creation skills and keep you at the forefront of educational innovation.

By implementing these action items and staying true to clarity, empowerment, and continuous growth, you will be well-equipped to create transformative courses that educate and inspire. Remember, your journey as a course creator is an ongoing discovery, adaptation, and refinement process. Embrace the challenges, celebrate the successes, and never stop striving to positively impact the lives of your learners, your community, and the world at large.

Shihan Sheriff is a 3X Best-Selling and International Award Winning Author, the Founder/CEO of MoneyMasterHQ.com, Host of Global Business Summit and Host of the podcast "The Money-Master HQ Show". You can connect with Shihan on LinkedIn via https://bit.ly/3YMVFTR

19

AVOID ABANDONMENT AND NO-SHOWS

BY ERNESTE CARLA ZIMMERMANN

Are online courses dead?

You may be asking yourself if it is worth the time and effort to create an amazing online course if you have also heard the rumors going around:

"The course market is too saturated."

"No one is buying courses anymore."

Rest assured, the e-learning industry is accelerating, and course creation is here to stay!

According to a report by Global Market Insights, the e-learning market size reached USD 399.3 billion in 2022 and is estimated to almost double by 2032. The global e-learning market has experienced remarkable growth because of a combination of technological advancements and the demand for accessible, flexible learning options, and the increased integration of AI.

The e-learning system nowadays is integrated in various industries, and even in the health sector, to cater to the growing demand for immersive learning and hands-on training.

For you as the course creator, the benefit of having an online course people can order any time without you being involved cannot be overestimated. It's an asset and marketing piece you create once. If done right, students will love and recommend it. This can lead not only to accelerated credibility, expert status, and authority in your niche but also to passive income while you are doing other things and enjoying life.

If you are a business owner like me, you're likely to be overwhelmed with all the tasks on your list, and one-on-one sessions will, over time, lead to exhaustion and severe health problems like burnout. I have been there, maxed out and exhausted.

Online course creation can make a huge difference for you! Yes, you still must put in the time and effort to create the course in the first place, but then you can automate the whole process of promotion, sales, and enrollment, and welcome your students all at once.

Shocking stats: 97 percent who purchase a course are likely to never complete it.

I'm sharing my lessons learned the hard way, so you don't have to go through trial and error to find out. Marisa Murgatroyd, a mentor of mine who created a platform and software named Xperiencify with inbuilt gamification, wondered why so many people didn't start or finish courses. She studied the abandonment rate. She found that only 3 percent of people who buy a course ever complete it, while 97 percent who purchase a course don't. If they don't finish the course, they won't get the desired outcome, and you won't be recommended. It's not likely they will ever buy from you again.

This software builds rapport with the student to increase the "know, like, and trust factor" and leads to addiction through fun and gamification. People love to play and be rewarded. And you don't need to be a programmer to insert this gimmick into your courses, as I'm not a techie myself.

I incorporate gamification and rewards in all my courses because I really want to have people benefit from it. Way too many course creators and coaches are only focused on making money. Otherwise, they would reach out if a student didn't log in or continue through the course.

I really care and want them to get to the next level in their lives. That's my deepest wish for them.

I also use quizzes and assessments as a lead magnet. People love to explore and rate themselves. It's a great way to get people to opt in to your list and serves as a Band-Aid. Once you contact them to reveal their results, they know themselves and you much better and are likely to sign up for your course to get the promised solution.

The best online course is one that stands out.

I needed help with how to start, what course to create, and how to incorporate personalization and gamification while catering to different learning styles. I highly recommend you focus on these two key ingredients of personalized gamification and catering to all learning styles right away to make sure you get the great results you anticipate.

Let me share what I consider to be the key elements of an online course that stands out:

1 **Uniqueness is Key**: Creating online courses that truly stand out in a crowded market is challenging. They have in common that they are unique and presented authentically. The hero's journey is about discovering, aligning, and leveraging our life's purpose, owning who we are, and living authentically and purposefully while exploring our full potential. Course creation is about aligning your expertise with the right opportunity and audience and delivering exceptional value for the students.

2 **Explore the topic** and foundation of your course by asking yourself:

○ What do I want to share with the world? Usually this is your superpower, gift, and unique expertise, skill, or passion.

○ What knowledge or transformation can you offer that sets you apart? In my case as a transformational life and business coach, I teach what I preach and have studied over decades or have lived through teaching moments myself (e.g., my near-death experience).

3 **Evaluate the market** opportunities and choose a suitable audience who needs your solutions. Explore their pain points and match your course to solve these problems, and then position your course to address those needs accordingly.

4 **Leverage, Freedom, and Impact**: Combine your course

with the right audience, and you'll unlock leverage, freedom, and impact. Leverage means reaching more people without working harder. Freedom allows you to design your lifestyle while your course is running and selling on autopilot. Impact comes from transforming lives through your content.

5 Adapt to the Changing Landscape: Today's learners expect more than just information, which they can easily get on the web on their own. They seek transformation and results. To stand out, your course must deliver a profound change or transformation.

6 Create a Transformational Course: Beyond information, focus on creating a course that truly transforms your students. Consider their pain points, learning preferences, and desired outcomes.

How do you implement what I prescribed?

Cater to all different learning styles, or no-shows and abandonment will be on the rise.

It's important to create content in various ways, such as audio, video, print, and engaging activities so you can cater to all different students. Additionally, you need to make them love to absorb the content with personalization and gamification, engage them in exercises, workbooks, and homework assignments, and measure and reveal their progress.

If your mission is to truly transform lives with your courses and transformational programs, you need to go even further and offer a community of peers and buddies to go on the transformational ride together, which will also be a place to insert implementation calls and hold their hands if needed.

A self-study online course on its own can't give students the handhold they need to set sail on a transformational journey. In this case, consider creating a hybrid to combine all aspects, like I do.

I use the educational "teach-sketch-review" presentation style to keep students engaged and hungry for more. Each piece of teaching (for the auditory learners) is followed by sketching something (for the visual learners) and then reviewing it with an engaging exercise where they implement the teaching (for the kinesthetics). Make sure they get a transcript so the readers and writers can follow along too.

The most important learning styles you must incorporate in your course creation are visual, auditory, kinesthetic, and reading and writing. You should also consider catering to solitary and linguistic learners.

Let me explain how you can implement this wisdom:

Visual learners love images, graphs, videos, etc. Make sure you insert visual elements in your course.

Auditory learners love to absorb the content while listening. You must provide audio for them. Additionally, students with another learning style might be using audio to listen to the content on the go while being in the car, gym, or doing something else.

Kinesthetic learners thrive when they can physically

engage with the material through movement, role-playing, hands-on activities, experiments, and interactive exercises.

Solitary learners really perform great in self-study courses, as they prefer a quiet environment.

Logical/analytical learners are the analytical left brainers, and they thrive on structure and logical sequences, and love problem-solving exercises and critical thinking tasks.

Linguistic learners love to engage in language-related activities such as discussions, debates, verbal expression, and storytelling.

Individuals may exhibit a combination of the learning styles mentioned. They are known as multimodal learners.

You as the course creator and educator can easily fail if you're not adapting your teaching methods to accommodate the different learning preferences. I had to learn this fact decades ago and have since incorporated this to all content I'm creating, like presentations, webinars, etc.

In fact, every podcast episode is recorded as MP4, MP3, and transcription, so I'm able to repurpose the content on all my stages, in my books, and on social media.

If I would be creating the course the way I am as a kinesthetic person and multimodal learner, I would repel a huge group of logical learners, writers, readers, and solitaries.

Which course type should you create?

I have decided to create a bunch of online courses at low- and mid-tier pricing on easily consumable topics focused on information that can be promoted with ads and in joint venture partnerships. People can click on the ad and automatically enroll, ready to start the course at their own pace without me being involved. That's amazing.

But this doesn't fit the audience who dares to transform their lives. So, on top of the online courses, I had to create the transformational signature programs, which are hybrids with high-tier pricing. For programs in a price range of $2,000 and above, students expect more than a self-learning course. We incorporate interactive elements where we provide personal support such as emergency calls, implementation calls, and hot seats, as well as laser coaching in group settings delivered on Zoom calls, to ensure that students can implement and transform.

My signature *Freestyle-Your-Life coaching systems* include the *Anxiety Freedom Formula* to mentor heart-centered business owners and help them break free from self-sabotaging patterns such as self-denial, self-betrayal, and self-oppression. I help them master their anxiety and fears and reveal how to restyle their lives and businesses so they can *live and lead fearlessly authentic by design* on their own terms!

The add-on signature program is the *Authenticity Blueprint*, helping entrepreneurs and especially health and wellness practitioners to live and lead authentically. The next-level programs are license and certification programs. I license my courses to health and wellness facilitators and practitioners to sell to their audiences, saving them from the need to create their own courses.

The best way to get ahead is to follow a proven system.

On all the Freestyle-Your-Life stages, such as the *FLY-*

Freestyle-Your-Life podcast, the *Freestyle-Your-Life online summits*, and in the *Freestyle-Your-Life books*, I'm inspiring and reminding entrepreneurs to discover their true nature within and to express their purpose as awakened leaders in the world. Once they have discovered their purpose and have mastered their anxiety and fears, they can live and lead fearlessly and authentically.

I always recommend an engaging and informative format. On the weekly *FLY-Freestyle-Your-Life podcast*, for example, episodes are available in audio, video, and written format and typically include:

1 **Interviews:** As the host, I interview inspiring guest experts from various fields, such as personal development, health, entrepreneurship, creativity, and happiness. These guests share their stories, insights, best shortcuts, and practical tips for implementation.

2 **Themes and Topics:** Episodes focus on specific themes, such as overcoming negative emotions, managing stress, and achieving personal freedom. Listeners gain actionable advice and strategies.

3 **Authentic Conversations:** The podcast encourages authentic conversations about life, growth, and self-mastery. It's a space where listeners can explore their own paths and learn from others' experiences. They can also reach out for assistance and comment in the *Authentically Me community* called *FLY-Nation*.

4 **Practical Takeaways:** Whether it's understanding anxiety symptoms, addressing burnout, or finding happi-

ness, each episode provides practical takeaways that listeners can apply to their lives.

This is just an example of how we incorporate course creation at *Freestyle-Your-Life*. As the process to become fearless and authentic by design is very transformational, we choose self-learning courses to deliver information and the hybrid course format to enhance change and transformation.

They need a mentor by their side to overcome the anxiety and fear to start and follow through. This is adaptable to almost everything when we start out. I had countless mentors in all areas of my life and business to learn the best and fastest way to get where I aim.

As Winston S. Churchill said, "Success is not final; failure is not fatal. It is the courage to continue that counts."

I encourage you to be a brave fire starter! Depending on your topic and niche, you can easily create a self-learning online course or adapt to hybrid course delivery. I wish you lots of fun in implementing personalization and gamification while catering to the specific learning styles of your audience.

Certified Life & Biz coach, multiple bestselling author, Podcast & Summit host, Creator of the FREESTLE-YOUR-LIFE Method®️ *helping heart-centered entrepreneurs to live & lead fearlessly authentic by design.,You can reach Erneste Carla at https:// freestyle-your-life.com/*

. . .

Certified Life & Biz coach, mult. bestselling author, Podcast &
Summit host, Creator of the FREESTLE-YOUR-LIFE
Method® helping heart-centered entrepreneurs to live &
lead fearlessly authentic by design. You can reach Erneste
Carla at https://freestyle-your-life.com/.

THE CO-AUTHOR PROJECT

Compiled By

co-author.me

13891947R00092